HEARTLAND

Poets of the Midwest

LUCIEN STRYK

Editor

NORTHERN ILLINOIS UNIVERSITY PRESS

De Kalb

ACKNOWLEDGMENT

ABELARD-SCHUMAN, New York: for "Religious Emphasis Week" and "For Damaris, About To Be Married" from *The Unknowing Dance*, by Chad Walsh (copyright 1964 by Chad Walsh). THE UNIVERSITY OF CHICAGO PRESS, Chicago: for "St. Louis Midday," "Hampton Road." "Late Shift In The Mill," "Old Moon Planter," "Church Of Rose Of Lima, Cincinnati," "Night Fire," "Edwardsville Before Sunrise," "North On One-Eleven," "Heman Avenue Holiday," and "June Night On The River," from *Rivers Into Islands*, by John Knoepfle (copyright 1965 by The University of Chicago). CORNELL UNIVERSITY PRESS, Ithaca: for "Elm Trees," "Terminal Theater," "Waldheim Cemetery," "All The Mornings," "Scenes From A Text," "My Students," "Miss Elderli Dora Des Moines — One March," and "Turnpike," from *Kissing The Dancer & Other Poems*, by Robert Sward. THE DIAL PRESS, New York: for "Wheel Of Summer," "Sacrifice Of The Sparrows Of The Field," and "Crane," from *The Wheel Of Summer*, by Joseph Langland (copyright 1963 by Joseph Langland). GROVE PRESS, New York: for "Recollection" and "Pagan Saturday," from *Cycle For Mother Cabrini*, by John Logan (copyright 1955 by John Logan). HARPER & ROW: PUBLISHERS, New York: for "The Snow Shovel," "Spiritual Biography," "Suburban Vista," "They Walk Under Ladders," and *from Eros and Agape from Eden Two-Way*," by Chad Walsh (copyright 1950 by Curtis Publishing Company, 1951, 1952, 1953, 1954 by Chad Walsh). "Negro Hero," "I Love Those Little Booths At Benvenuti's" "A Man Of The Middle Class," and "The Sundays Of Satin-Legs Smith," from *Selected Poems* by Gwendolyn Brooks (copyright 1945, 1949, 1960 by Gwendolyn Brooks Blakely). "Prairie Town," "Tornado," "Conservative," "In Response To A Question," "Before The Big Storm," "The Only Card I Got On My Birthday Was From An Insurance Man," "Adults Only," "Time's Exile," "Long Distance," and "The Peters Family," from *Traveling Through The Dark*, by William Stafford (copyright 1951, 1954, 1956, 1957, 1958, 1959, 1960, 1961, 1962, by William Stafford. HEARSE PRESS, Eureka, California: for "Like In The Movies" and "Love Lies A-Bleeding," from *Hot & Cold: Running*, by Frederick Eckman. HOUGHTON MIFFLIN COMPANY, Boston: for "West Of Childhood," "Of Flesh And Bone," "The Widow's Yard," "Part Of The Darkness," "Children Are Game," "The Milkman," "Letter From Slough Pond," and "This Room Is Full Of Clocks," from *West Of Childhood*, by Isabella Gardner (copyright 1965 by Houghton Mifflin Company); "A Poem For Home," "No Voyage," "Beyond The Snow Belt," "How I Went Truant From School To Visit A River," "Dancers At Banstead," "A Letter From Home," "After My Grandfather's Death: A Poem Of The China Clock," and "Anton and Yaro," from *No Voyage And Other Poems*, by Mary Oliver (copyright 1965 by Mary Oliver). INDIANA UNIVERSITY PRESS, Bloomington: for "The Visits Of My Aunt," "Bert In The Orchard," "Night Constable," "The Last Resort," and "The Deaths At Paragon, Indiana," from *The Deaths At Paragon, Indiana*, by John Woods (copyright 1955 by John Woods). UNIVERSITY OF NEBRASKA PRESS, Lincoln: for "The Fires Of Life," "Ox Driver," "From A Naturalist's Notebook: Smoke," "The Cimarron," "Letter From Fort Scott" and "The Language Of Yes," from *The Year Of The Green Wave*, by Bruce Cutler (copyright 1960 by University of Nebraska Press); "Where We Are" and "Sun City," from *Sun City*, by Bruce Cutler (copyright 1964 by University of Nebraska Press); "The Hometown Hero Comes Home," "Wedding Day," "Words For A Friend Who Was Accidentally Shot While Hunting Pheasants In Northern Iowa," "Invitation To A Young River Queen," "Two Dreams Of Kansas," "Hollyhocks," "Two Beers In Argyle, Wisconsin," "Fragments From An Illinois Scrapbook," "The Forgotten Graveyard," and

---

Manufactured in the United States of America

CONTENTS

INTRODUCTION

M u c h as he is tempted to skirt it, there is a question, prickling and persistent, that anyone editing a book of this type must try to answer: In this time of shifting values and great human mobility is there a true midland, or for that matter any other, regional literature? Writing on "The Reality of Midwestern Literature," * John T. Flanagan has this to say:

The twelve states that compose the area today are probably the most heterogeneous group in terms of population in the entire union. Virtually every country of Europe has sent sizable contingents of settlers to the heartland of America. Foreign-born and second-generation citizens are still so common today that we normally think of Grand Rapids as a Dutch community, Minneapolis as Scandinavian, and Milwaukee and Cincinnati as German cities, while metropolises like Detroit and Chicago seem sometimes to be loosely joined islands of national groups ranging from the Poles and the Jews to the Irish and the Negroes. Can any distinctive, clearly defined literature with recognizable themes and qualities develop from such a turmoil?

Mr. Flanagan thinks that there is a literature identifiable as midwestern, and he goes on to say that writers of the region "won distinction in spite of their style rather than because of it . . . Style to them was generally a means, not an end in itself. As a consequence, the work they produced has enormous vigor and impact; it is rarely aesthetically pleasing."

It would appear that Mr. Flanagan has doubts about the quality of some midland writing. As to the charge

---

*The Midwest: Myth or Reality? Thomas T. McAvoy, C.S.C. (ed.), University of Notre Dame Press, 1961.

that the writing of the region is "rarely aesthetically pleasing," as if that were art's purpose and not the expression of inner reality, listen to Sherwood Anderson, in "An Apology for Crudity":

For a long time I have believed that crudity is an inevitable quality in the production of really significant present-day literature. How indeed is one to escape the obvious fact that there is as yet no native subtlety of thought or living among us? And if we are a crude and childlike people how can our literature hope to escape the influence of that fact? Why indeed should we want it to escape? . . . Why should we Americans aspire to an appearance of subtlety that belongs not to us but to old lands and places? Why talk of intellectuality . . . when we have not accepted the life we have?

The awakening to the reality of "the life we have" has been responsible in great measure for the strength of midwestern poetry as well as prose, and Edgar Lee Masters, who became a good poet only after he stopped being a poor emulator of British poets, is an early example of what has since happened to developing artists repeatedly. Sometimes, as in the case of Karl Shapiro, whose first work was cunningly crafted as that of any of his British contemporaries, there are surprising conversions. Elsewhere, as with Paul Engle, there is a tension that seems to result from divided loyalties, but it is a tension which makes for convincing poetry.

THERE are perhaps as many reasons against a book of this kind as for it, so it may be a good thing to tell at the outset why another anthology was made. For a number of years now a strong, varied poetry has been written in, and often about, midland America, a poetry which owes little or nothing to the example and achieve-

ment of those figures always associated with the region —
Sandburg, Masters, Lindsay. The main purpose of this
volume is to present generous samples of such poetry,
whether or not it derives from and appears to continue
the old "Evergreen Tradition," as it is sometimes called.

The heartland is not difficult to define, and as a
geopolitical unit it has much in common with the heart-
lands of other continents. It is made up of Ohio, Michigan,
Missouri, Indiana, Illinois, Wisconsin, Minnesota, Kan-
sas, Nebraska, Iowa, and the Dakotas. The most fertile
in the country, roughly half of the region is essentially
agrarian. The plain is its distinguishing topographic
feature, and its prairies have helped shape its arts and
architecture. One thinks of the frame house, the grain
elevator, even the skyscraper as midwestern; and it was
Frank Lloyd Wright's idea that the building arts should
utilize local earth and stone, that the skyscraper should
be raised only in a place where it can cast an unbroken
shadow.

John Steinbeck has made an interesting observation: [*]
There is no question in my mind that places in America mark
their natives, not only in their speech patterns, but physically
— in build, in stance, in conformation. Climate may have
something to do with this as well as food supply and tech-
niques of living; in any case, each of us can detect a stranger.
In the heartland there is, for example, a sense of isolation
many, especially its artists, seem to feel. It is a feeling
expressed graphically in a number of poems in this
book. But to my mind no one has expressed it better
recently than a poet of the Pacific northwest, Richard
Hugo, in a piece called "In Stafford Country":

---

[*]"America and the Americans," *Saturday Evening Post*, July 2, 1966

No hills. Raw wind unchecked, brings word
of death from Texas. No shade. Sun bruises
the oats gold. With homes exposed
no wonder people love. Farms absorb
the quiet of the snow, and birds
are black and nameless miles away.

Without a shield of hills, a barricade
of elms, one resorts to magic, hiding
the joker well behind the gesturing hand.
Childish wars continue in our minds.
Paint is the gray it was in Carthage.

Where land is flat, words are far apart.
Each word is seen, coming from far off,
a calm storm, almost familiar, across
the plain. The word floats by, alive.
Homes are empty and the love goes on
as the odor of grain jumps in the wind.

It is my hope that a clear sense of the region, in all its
diversity, as well as its people, will emerge from the
poetry in *Heartland: Poets of the Midwest.*

The book has other purposes, foremost among them
to give pleasure, but there is one that I should like
to mention at once. As a teacher of poetry, I have been
conscious for some time of the possibilities of a volume
like this, and to a degree that helped determine the kind
of verse that went into it. The reader will notice, for
instance, that there is both narrative and meditative
writing (that of Robert Huff and Joseph Langland being
good examples of the former, Elder Olson's of the
latter), and various approaches to the making of the
poem, from the use of rhyme and traditional stanza pat-
terns, as in the work of John F. Nims and Chad Walsh,

to the highly imagistic, free-associative method of John Knoepfle, James Tate, and Dave Etter, among others. And in Karl Shapiro's work there is something new, at least in this country, a vigorous prose-poetry.

Though certain poems (John Woods', for example) appear to reveal a continued interest in figures such as Masters, and whereas others like James Hearst's seem rather old-fashioned in their simplicity and lyricism, there is not a poem in the book that I would consider dated in method and effect. Many are written in a style that for want of a better term might be called "international," using methods such as surrealism freely, a style aware of the best contemporary European, Latin American, and Oriental poetry. Outstanding examples of this kind of poem are Paul Carroll's long piece, and much of the work of Robert Bly, Isabella Gardner, John Logan, Robert Sward, and James Wright.

I T S E E M E D to me when selecting poems that it would be foolish to insist that all of them be set in the midwest, if only because that could induce a kind of claustrophobia. Yet, unless most of them turned out to be of that type, the book was in danger of becoming just another characterless and thus unnecessary anthology. I have myself been an uneasy reader of anthologies, and I wanted to avoid giving the book the miscellaneous, unfocused feel most of them seem to have. So far as the poets themselves are concerned, I knew that certain conditions would have to be set down at once if things were to be kept manageable: contributors would have to be living writers; they would either have to be from the midwest or have long and firm ties with the area. And they would

have to have written a fair amount of poetry set in it.
Surprisingly or not, a number of fine poets from the
region, and others still residing there, have not written
about it.

It is common apparently for editors of books like this
to indulge in excuses, apologies, and disclaimers. I will
say only this much, while accepting full responsibility
for any shortcomings the book may have: with the help
of a few impartial critics, I made out a list of poets
whose work was considered indispensable to the volume,
keeping in mind the need to present a variety of styles.
I then began looking through periodicals for suitable
work by writers I admire, but who have not yet pub-
lished a volume. With the list completed, I wrote the
poets, and all of them responded enthusiastically. Finally
came the task of selecting poems from the many books
I looked over, and, put simply as possible, I chose only
poems I liked.

If the book could have been longer, which it could
not, and if each poet's section could have been shorter,
which seemed to me unwise, then the work of more
good midland poets would have been included. I wanted
especially to avoid the buckshot approach, single poems
by numerous poets resulting in chaos, yet I am very
much aware of the possibility that through ignorance or
oversight I have not included work by poets the equal of
any in the book. Another factor in my selection was that
I wanted the book to have something like an urban-rural
balance, and with that in mind a few poets were left out
simply because their work would have tipped that
balance.

In its balance at least, this volume can claim some
distinction. Rarely in regional collections is the city

given its proper due, and my hope was that by using a goodly number of urban poems a truer picture of the midwest would be presented. Surely, when an authoritative account of modern American poetry is written, space will be given the poet's adjustment to the metropolis, the impact of which has been often blamed for the decline of his art. Hart Crane, perhaps the midland's greatest urban poet, saw more clearly than any of his contemporaries the danger to poetry of ignoring the machine and, by extension, urban experience. He writes:*
For unless poetry can absorb the machine, i.e., *acclimatize* it as naturally and casually as trees, galleons, castles and all other human associations of the past, then poetry has failed of its full contemporary function. This process does not infer any program of lyrical pandering to the taste of those obsessed by the importance of machinery; nor does it essentially involve even the specific mention of a single mechanical contrivance. It demands, however, along with the traditional qualifications of the poet, an extraordinary capacity for surrender, at least temporarily, to the sensations of urban life.

Yet many poets have expressed concern about the encroachment of the city upon their rural if not pastoral domain, while others have shown disdain for the city by refusing to admit into their work its commonest trappings: cars, factories, and so on. And others have loathed it. Robinson Jeffers, though no midwesterner, had a vision in his fine but life-despising poem "November Surf" of "The cities gone down, the people fewer and the hawks more numerous." All this may be regrettable, but it is a fact that the struggle to absorb the machine and the city is often keen. Because they are engaged in that

---

*"Modern Poetry," *The Collected Poems of Hart Crane,* Liveright Publishing Corp., 1933.

struggle, the urban poetry of Thomas McGrath, Elder Olson, John F. Nims, and others has some significance.

P LANNING the book, I felt that one of its most important purposes would be to offer proof that what appears to many a colorless region is to some rich, complicated, thrilling. That, in short, the midwest is made up of the stuff of poetry. And once those living in it begin to see its details — cornfields, skyscrapers, small-town streets, whatever — with the help of their poets, they will find it not only more possible to live with some measure of contentment among its particulars but even, miraculously, begin to love them and the poems they fill. Perhaps that is being quixotic, but if good art needs justification, surely the fact that it is capable of inspiring reverence for the things it celebrates, for the insights it offers, is justification enough.

If read as they should be read, the poems of R. R. Cuscaden will open the reader's eyes to the humanity of the small railroad towns of the heartland; those of William Stafford and Bruce Cutler make him see Kansas, that wheaty yawn somewhere west of Chicago, as a place men can love desperately; while the poems of Paul Engle and James Hearst about Iowa cornfields, among other things, make the reader comprehend that what he had thought to be merely a relentlessly rising territory — impossible to see through or over any summer — is a place where lives are bravely lived. And what of the northern woods, which most consider just so much timber? Perhaps the work of Parm Mayer, Robert Huff, and Dennis Schmitz in this volume will make it impossible to see them as that again. Quixotic or not, that is the hope, and it has been my experience that those normally hostile to poetry will often respond, some with alacrity, to poems dealing with their world.

It struck me as the book was being completed that its poets love this region, though sometimes, such being its nature, that love is disguised as its opposite. It may be that the affection its poets have for the heartland is the sort a parent will have for the homelier or less endowed child. In any case, no one who has seen other parts of this country will claim that the midwest compares in natural beauty with, say, the Pacific northwest or New England. Yet the region does have characteristic beauty — the lake and river country, the roll of southern Indiana, the sharp dense feel of the northern woods. And so far as much of the rest is concerned, if the poet is worth his salt he is certain to get as much out of it as those who live elsewhere get from mountains and the sea. For what the land does not supply, his imagination will, and from the synthesis can come things rich and strange, as in Joseph Langland's remarkable "The Wheel of Summer," the first stanza of which goes:

> The dark land rose in the luminous arch of sky.
> The bald sun softly grew. Down by the barn
> My father and we three sons watched how it fell
> Through hazes of sour dust by the old pig pens.
> "They got away from us," my father said.
> He didn't need to say it. The great sun god
> Bowed to the grassy sea by the western hills,
> Darkened to blood, rolled in the tasseled corn
> And flamed our blinking eyeballs. "Yup," we said,
> And turned in the dirty twilight to our thoughts.

Yet midwesterners are often defensive about
their region, and on occasion this leads to extravagant
claims for it, boostering. For example, Louis H. Sullivan,
founder of the Chicago school of architecture and a great
artist, is reported to have said, "New York is not the
country. It is in this land physically to be sure, but
spiritually it is on the outskirts." Often spoken of as the
Second City, conscious of competing in its big-shouldered
way with just about every other American city, Chicago
is sometimes provincially defensive, especially when it
comes to the arts. But there is little doubt that part of
its (as well as other midland cities') suspicion of the east
is due to the feeling that its cult of the common man, as
in Sandburg, is little understood, let alone admired, back
there.

It is tempting to dismiss the discussion of such atti-
tudes as generality, yet occasionally something will come
up to demonstrate all too clearly that they do indeed
exist. Take the well-known Harold Painter custody case,
which concerned not an easterner but a westerner, and
one no less "foreign" for that. In the opinion of many,
the Supreme Court of Iowa in its unanimous decision
to grant custody of Painter's son to his maternal grand-
parents, thereby denying the father his natural rights,
was acting on sound midwestern principles. Damaging
to his cause, for example, was an interest in Zen Bud-
dhism. A child psychologist retained by the grandparents,
called the father "a romantic and somewhat of a dreamer,"
and though the trial judge disregarded the psychologist's
testimony as "exaggerated" and ruled for the father, the
higher court reversed the ruling. It refused to find the

father unfit in any legal sense, instead compared the two homes offered the boy, finding the Iowa home "dependable, conventional, middle-class, Middle West" and the father's "romantic, impractical, and unstable." The assumption was that Harold Painter, a political liberal and possibly an atheist to boot, would provide a home for his son that was, to use the court's language, "unconventional, arty, Bohemian, and probably intellectually stimulating."

Perhaps it does not matter, except for the boy, whether Mr. Painter was in reality an unstable drifter, but it seems to me that it matters very much that the highest court of the state recognized such categories of personality and gave them legal sanction. Laws confirm customs established by usage. They also, on occasion, parody the very principles of morality they are meant to crystallize. In any case, nothing could illustrate better the mistrust of the poetry of life that is sometimes felt in the midwest. Greater honor to its poets, then, for finding it possible to dream in towns like Ames, Iowa.

Still another good reason for regional anthologies is the possibility of bringing together poets who have best expressed their area. In planning a book around their achievement, however humble, however lacking in reputation they may be, for once one can afford to pass by a number of those stars and heavies who form the national poetic establishment. This book is not an attempt to provincialize poetry, and I dare say it has its share of "names," but there are represented with equal or more space poets who have not yet published volumes, and some of the work has not had magazine publication. So far as the "name" poets are concerned, they are included because in my judgment they fully deserve the reputations they have and, more important, because they have written good poems with midland settings.

In spite of all that I have been saying about the importance to the volume of regional awareness, for the poet there is normally very little interest in region as such. What matters to him is the manner in which the details of his world — be they silos, backyards, or city corners — affect his inner life. The poet is rarely interested in concepts. Though the midwest has sometimes been thought politically progressive, the region of Veblen, LaFolette, and Altgeld, it is not to be wondered that a poet such as Gwendolyn Brooks, compassionately involved in the starved lives of her people, should see it as an altogether different sort of place. Yet if midwestern poetry does have a special quality, it probably is to be found in its largeness of vision.

Because most of its poets live close to the earth, the poetry of this region is suggestive of the character of its life. In the work of Mary Oliver one feels longing, and a nostalgia without sentimentality, for the purer world of an Ohio childhood; in that of Lisel Mueller the hunger for creative fulfillment in a limiting environment; in Joseph Langland's the fears and ecstasies of growing up on a farm; in Parm Mayer's a joyous, almost frontiersman's independence, and so on. If it is as true of the heartland as elsewhere that the farms are being deserted for the cities, then the poems of Thomas McGrath about uprooted men in the cities have an importance beyond all graphs. But not all poets of the region seem to be caught up in its changes or feel its stunting urgencies. Dennis Schmitz has the mystic's awe of nature, as have Robert Huff and James Hearst, and that is as much a part of the midland experience as was Thoreau's of New England.

Many midwesterners live in small towns of the kind Sinclair Lewis made synonymous with emptiness, and Babbittry is everywhere encountered, yet the small-town poets in the book find it possible to love what even Sinclair Lewis could not fully hate. Frederick Eckman's poems show that the pressures of that life cannot crush the poetry in a man, R. R. Cuscaden's that however small the town, it can be a place of loss and pathos, Dave Etter's that what most see as drab has a wacky pace and color worthy of a Chagall, and Raymond Roseliep's that it can be the source of an exultant spiritual life. In these poets, in the work of John Woods, Chad Walsh, and others, there is affection for the small town, as well as a keen sense of its cultural poverty. But if it is true that poets are the antennae they are sometimes grudgingly called, this is not surprising. Certainly we must continue to look to them for those sensitive images that sustain us. And if the poets of the heartland see their territory as often luminous and wild, are we to conclude that the weary passer-through who views it as a terrible sameness may, in fact, be seeing nothing other than himself?

THINKING of the diversity of styles to be found in this book, it would appear that the struggle between the formal and the free, the cooked and the raw, goes on, nowhere more than in the heartland. And everyone involved in the writing and serious reading of the new poetry seems to be engaged in it. At times, when it reaches a peak, one is tempted to dismiss it as so much thunder, recalling that every utterance has its own form, suitable or unsuitable as the case may be. But that would be playing ostrich, for those involved, among them the best of our poets, have great influence and passionate concern for the future of American verse. They have formed schools demanding rigorous discipleship, and are acidic in the criticism of each other.

By one such school, some of whose adherents are from the midwest, rhyme and regular stanzas, once considered to be methods of control and stimulators of the imagination, at least by expert employers of them, are seen as hindrances if not cardinal sins. But surely there is no need to remind anyone that distinguished formal poems have been written by Yeats, Crane, Thomas, and, thinking of poets in this volume, Paul Engle, John F. Nims, and William Stafford among others. Things have become very simple. Writing a certain kind of poem these days is like holding out the red cape, and since poets are rarely nimble on their feet, they are often gored. Of course it is always possible to become a cow.

Whether a poem is memorable or forgettable is still the only question worth asking. If unsuccessful "formal" poems resemble knocking engines, unsuccessful "free" poems are like trays of junk jewelry onto which, though not always, a few real gems have been dropped. But the upholders of the free are on the warpath, and recent American criticism, at least that taken most seriously by young writers, is dominated by them. Karl Shapiro, William Carlos Williams, Charles Olson and a number of others have spoken out, from different points of view, against tradition, and much of what they have said has been demonstrably compelling to another generation.

In an introduction to Bruce Cutler's first volume, *The Year of the Green Wave*, Karl Shapiro recalls Sherwood Anderson:

It is true that we have many poetry books year by year, that literary journals . . . open their pages to poets, that . . . prizes are awarded and honors bestowed upon American poets. It is true that we have lowbrow, middlebrow, and highbrow poets . . . Yet it is almost impossible to distinguish our poetry from the British, or, when it is translated, from the French, Italian, Spanish, etc., of our time. A poetic standardization has set in and the separate voice has been lost — even the separate national voice. There is, after all, an American voice which is completely distinct . . . And there is an American place which is unique and has a spirit of its own. But there is practically no poetry to express this place and use this voice . . . We are not aiming at "patriotic" or "regional" verse but at something truer: the voice of the American and everything good and bad contained in that . . . word. Our verse now is either pure decorum . . . or pure howling — either esthetic exercise or historical caterwauling. It wants breadth and above-ness; it want perspective and serenity; for it lacks both sensitivity and guts.

These are rousing words, and Karl Shapiro is one of the few who practice well what they preach, as can be seen in the selections in this book from *The Bourgeois Poet*, which while Whitmanesque in spirit has been described by some as a breakthrough in poetry. Yet it seems to me that the eye is one with that it sees, whether it sees formally or freely. In other words it may be part of the "bad" contained in the word American, in the American himself, that he is often not pure, that his voice has a French, Italian, or Spanish accent. For better

or worse it is still his voice, and one sometimes worth
listening to.

When choosing poems for this volume I was interested
not so much in the true midland voice, whatever that
might be, but in the chorus that a structured variety
of voices forms. And if the result is less a concert than
a Babel, at least all sorts of fine voices are being heard.
Put simply, without any particular aesthetic in mind, I
searched for — and feel that I found in abundance —
good poems set in the midwest.

A ND yet not to face certain critical issues posed by
the preceding discussion of tradition, freedom, etc.,
would be less than honest. In my view the most interest-
ing recent poetry is that being written by those fully
aware of the direction modernism is taking in world
literature. In a now famous review-essay printed in the
second issue of John Logan's magazine, *Choice,* Robert
Bly expresses himself as less concerned with the bad
formal poem (though some are discussed) than with an
altogether new kind of poem:
Poetry, by breaking up the stanza and moving toward in-
wardness, is creating for itself a way of expression open to
new thought. It is creating for itself an instrument of know-
ledge, a poem, responsive entirely to the imagination. Poetry's
purpose in growing is to advance deeper into the unknown
country. This is why the question of audience is irrelevant.
In order to penetrate into this country poetry must learn to
sleep differently, to awake differently, to listen to new sounds,
to walk differently.

*   *   *

All around us are huge reservoirs of bypassed emotions,
ignored feelings, unexplained thoughts. As Rilke said to

sculptors, there are hundreds of gestures being made which we are not aware of. The purpose of poetry is to awaken the half of us that has been asleep for many years — to express thoughts not yet thought. All expression of hidden feelings involves opposition to the existing order.

Robert Bly and others represented in this book are finding specimens of that poetry in the work of Europeans, Latin Americans, and Orientals. Also they are involved in the translation of such poems. But the most impressive thing about these writers is the way their explorations are affecting their own work and the judgment of their contemporaries. Their internationalism has quite naturally turned some of the poets against much of the verse written around them, and yet, how to explain that most of their work is regional in feeling? In a very curious manner the interest of these writers, along with others like Louis Simpson and W. S. Merwin, in modernist movements throughout the world, from that of the expressionist work of Georg Trakl to contemporary Zen poetry, has led them to center on immediate surroundings. Donald Hall, himself involved in the writing of it, has also described this new kind of poetry:*

The movement which seems to me *new* is subjective but not autobiographical. It reveals through images not particular pain, but general subjective life. This universal subjective corresponds to the old objective life of shared experience and knowledge. People can talk to each other most deeply in images. To read a poem of this sort, you must not try to translate the images into abstractions. They won't go. You must try to be open to them, to let them take you over and speak in their own language of feeling. It is the intricate

---

Contemporary American Poetry, Donald Hall (ed.), Penguin Books, 1962.

darkness of feeling and instinct which these poems mostly communicate.

The instinctual life cannot be expressed in abstractions; thus the concentration in such poetry on the personal world. Much of the finest poetry being written today has, whatever the poet's intention, a regional quality. That the area most prominent in the new poetry happens to be the midwest, is simply due to the fact that its most important makers, certainly its theorists, are from the area.

James Wright is one of these, and in the development of his work, from *The Green Wall* through *Saint Judas* to his last volume, *The Branch Will Not Break*, one can trace the advance of what many consider to be the most profound of the new American poetry. Good as they are, for what they are, stanzas such as the following, from "Autumnal," are common in the first volume:

> Soft, where the shadow glides,
> The yellow pears fall down.
> The long bough slowly rides
> The air of my delight.
>
> Air, though but nothing, air
> Falls heavy down your shoulder.
> You hold in burdened hair
> The color of my delight.

In his second volume, published two years later, in 1959, the poet is working more intensely, yet for the most part in as formal a way. Here is the title poem, the sonnet "Saint Judas":

> When I went out to kill myself, I caught
> A pack of hoodlums beating up a man.
> Running to spare his suffering, I forgot
> My name, my number, how my day began,

How soldiers milled around the garden stone
And sang amusing songs; how all that day
Their javelins measured crowds; how I alone
Bargained the proper coins, and slipped away.

Banished from heaven, I found this victim beaten,
Stripped, kneed, and left to cry. Dropping my rope
Aside, I ran, ignored the uniforms:
Then I remembered bread my flesh had eaten,
The kiss that ate my flesh. Flayed without hope,
I held the man for nothing in my arms.

This is a powerful dramatic monologue, tense with the moral ambiguity that has always seemed to interest the writer. The point of presenting it here is not to demonstrate that he writes the kind of free poem appearing on the last pages of this book because he is incapable of doing formal poems, but to show how great a transformation his work has undergone. Like that of the other poets with whom he is frequently grouped, his has been a willed journey, an earned liberation, and its most important stage took place between the appearance of *Saint Judas* and that of *The Branch Will Not Break* in 1963.

Selecting poems from James Wright's last volume was by far the easiest and at the same time most difficult editorial task I faced, for everything in it seemed for one reason or another suitable. In the years between the publication of his last two books the poet must have meditated long and rigorously, and one result has been a full involvement in his time and place. That it is the midwest is, of course, little more than coincidence, yet of great value to the art of the region. Along with the other poets in *Heartland: Poets of the Midwest,* James Wright has chosen not to ignore the land he stands on, finding it sufficient to his needs as man and artist.

It is very far from the purpose of this volume to up the midwest or claim superiority for its poetry, yet I am confident that the work done in the region today is in every way as distinguished as that done elsewhere, and that it is as representative as that written by those figures of the immediate past invariably associated with the region. A new generation of writers both sees and must be seen with different eyes. The vision of the midwest provided by the poems in this book, fragmented as it must be in our time, is perhaps imperfect, but it is no mirage. It is of a real place, and real poets offer it.

This book is dedicated to Charles Newman, editor of Northwestern University's *Tri-Quarterly*, and to my colleagues and students, former and present, at Northern Illinois University, who have encouraged me to believe that poetry of the kind that makes it up is important to their lives. The book could not have come into being without the interest and expert aid of J. M. Barker, director of Northern Illinois University Press. To him my profound thanks and gratitude. I am also grateful to my colleagues William Seat and Louis Glorfeld for valuable suggestions for the Introduction.

LUCIEN STRYK

ROBERT BLY, *editor and translator as well as poet, lives on a farm near Madison, Minnesota, in the region where he was born.* He *was educated at Harvard University and elsewhere, and he has received important grants, including the Guggenheim in poetry. Through his quarterly journal* The Sixties, *he has introduced to American readers many of the new poets of South America and Europe. His work has been published in anthologies and in most of the leading periodicals, including* Poetry Magazine, Choice, The Nation, Botteghe Oscure, *and* Hudson, Paris *and* San Francisco *reviews.* Silence in the Snowy Fields, *his first volume, appeared in 1962.*

THREE KINDS OF PLEASURES

I

Sometimes, riding in a car, in Wisconsin
Or Illinois, you notice those dark telephone poles
One by one lift themselves out of the fence line
And slowly leap on the gray sky —
And past them, the snowy fields.

II

The darkness drifts down like snow on the picked
    cornfields
In Wisconsin: and on these black trees
Scattered, one by one,
Through the winter fields —
We see stiff weeds and brownish stubble,
And white snow left now only in the wheeltracks of the
    combine.

III

It is a pleasure, also, to be driving
Toward Chicago, near dark,
And see the lights in the barns.
The bare trees more dignified than ever,
Like a fierce man on his deathbed,
And the ditches along the road half full of a private
    snow.

HUNTING PHEASANTS
IN A CORNFIELD

I

What is so strange about a tree alone in an open field?
It is a willow-tree. I walk around and around it.
The body is strangely torn, and cannot leave it.
At last I sit down beneath it.

II

It is a willow tree alone in acres of dry corn.
Its leaves are scattered around its trunk, and around me,
Brown now, and speckled with delicate black.
Only the cornstalks now can make a noise.

III

The sun is cold, burning through the frosty distances of
    space.
The weeds are frozen to death long ago.
Why then do I love to watch
The sun moving on the chill skin of the branches?

IV

The mind has shed leaves alone for years.
It stands apart with small creatures near its roots.
I am happy in this ancient place,
A spot easily caught sight of above the corn,
If I were a young animal ready to turn home at dusk.

DRIVING TOWARD THE LAC QUI PARLE RIVER

I

I am driving; it is dusk; Minnesota.
The stubble field catches the last growth of sun.
The soybeans are breathing on all sides.
Old men are sitting before their houses on carseats
In the small towns. I am happy,
The moon rising about the turkey sheds.

II

The small world of the car
Plunges through the deep fields of the night,
On the road from Willmar to Milan.
This solitude covered with iron
Moves through the fields of night
Penetrated by the noise of crickets.

III

Nearly to Milan, suddenly a small bridge,
And water kneeling in the moonlight.
In small towns the houses are built right on the ground;
The lamplight falls on all fours in the grass.
When I reach the river, the full moon covers it;
A few people are talking low in a boat.

POEM IN THREE PARTS

I
Oh, on an early morning I think I shall live forever!
I am wrapped in my joyful flesh,
As the grass is wrapped in its clouds of green.

II
Rising from a bed, where I dreamt
Of long rides past castles and hot coals,
The sun lies happily on my knees;
I have suffered and survived the night
Bathed in dark water, like any blade of grass.

III
The strong leaves of the box-elder tree,
Plunging in the wind, call us to disappear
Into the wilds of the universe,
Where we shall sit at the foot of a plant,
And live forever, like the dust.

DEPRESSION

I felt my heart beat like an engine high in the air,
Like those scaffolding engines standing only on planks;
My body hung about me'like an old grain elevator,
Useless, clogged, full of blackened wheat.
My body was sour, my life dishonest, and I fell asleep.

I dreamt that men came toward me, carrying thin wires;
I felt the wires pass in, like fire; they were old Tibetans,
Dressed in padded clothes, to keep out cold;
Then three work gloves, lying fingers to fingers,
In a circle, came toward me, and I awoke.

Now I want to go back among the dark roots;
Now I want to see the day pulling its long wing;
I want to see nothing more than two feet high;
I want to see no one, I want to say nothing,
I want to go down and rest in the black earth of silence.

WATERING THE HORSE

How strange to think of giving up all ambition!
Suddenly I see with such clear eyes
The white flake of snow
That has just fallen in the horse's mane!

THE CLEAR AIR OF OCTOBER

I can see outside the gold wings without birds
Flying around, and the wells of cold water
Without walls standing eighty feet up in the air,
I can feel the crickets' singing carrying them into the sky.

I know these cold shadows are falling for hundreds of
    miles,
Crossing lawns in tiny towns, and the doors of Catholic
    churches;
I know the horse of darkness is riding fast to the east,
Carrying a thin man with no coat.

And I know the sun is sinking down great stairs,
Like an executioner with a great blade walking into a
    cellar,
And the gold animals, the lions, and the zebras, and the
    pheasants,
Are waiting at the head of the stairs with robbers' eyes.

LAZINESS AND SILENCE

I

On a Saturday afternoon in the football season,
I lie in a bed near the lake,
And dream of moles with golden wings.

While the depth of the water trembles on the ceiling,
Like the tail of an enraged bird,
I watch the dust floating above the bed, content.

I think of ships leaving lonely harbors,
Dolphins playing far at sea,
Fish with the faces of old men come in from a blizzard.

II

A dream of moles with golden wings
Is not so bad; it is like imagining
Waterfalls of stone deep in mountains,
Or a wing flying alone beneath the earth.

I know that far out in the Minnesota lake
Fish are nosing the mouths of cold springs,
Whose water causes ripples in the sleeping sand,
Like a spirit moving in a body.

It is Saturday afternoon. Crowds are gathered,
Warmed by the sun, and the pure air.
I thought of this strange mole this morning,
After sleeping all night by the lake.

AFTER DRINKING ALL NIGHT WITH A FRIEND, WE GO OUT IN A BOAT AT DAWN TO SEE WHO CAN WRITE THE BEST POEM

These pines, these fall oaks, these rocks,
This water dark and touched by wind —
I am like you, you dark boat,
Drifting over water fed by cool springs.

Beneath the waters, since I was a boy,
I have dreamt of strange and dark treasures,
Not of gold, or strange stones, but the true
Gift, beneath the pale lakes of Minnesota.

This morning also, drifting in the dawn wind,
I sense my hands, and my shoes, and this ink —
Drifting, as all of this body drifts,
Above the clouds of the flesh and the stone.

A few friendships, a few dawns, a few glimpses of grass,
A few oars weathered by the snow and the heat,
So we drift toward shore, over cold waters,
No longer caring if we drift or go straight.

GWENDOLYN BROOKS *was born in Topeka, Kansas, but has lived most of her life in Chicago. Before the publication in 1945 of her first book of poetry* A Street In Bronzeville *she was the recipient of four Poetry Workshop Awards given by the Midwestern Writers' Conference. She has held two Guggenheim Fellowships, the* Mademoiselle Merit Award, *an award by the Academy of Arts and Letters, the Eunice Tietjens Memorial Award by* Poetry Magazine. *In 1950, for Annie Allen, she won the Pulitzer Prize. She has also written* Bronzeville Boys and Girls *(for children),* The Bean Eaters, Selected Poems, *and a work of fiction,* Maud Martha.

NEGRO HERO
to suggest Dorie Miller

I had to kick their law into their teeth in order to save
   them.
However I have heard that sometimes you have to deal
Devilishly with drowning men in order to swim them to
   shore.
Or they will haul themselves and you to the trash and
   the fish beneath.
(When I think of this, I do not worry about a few
Chipped teeth.)

It is good I gave glory, it is good I put gold on their
   name.
Or there would have been spikes in the afterward hands.
But let us speak only of my success and the pictures in
   the Caucasian dailies

As well as the Negro weeklies. For I am a gem.
(They are not concerned that it was hardly The Enemy
       my fight was against
but them.)

It was a tall time. And of course my blood was
Boiling about in my head and straining and howling and
       singing me on.

Of course I was rolled on wheels of my boy itch to get
       at the gun.
Of course all the delicate rehearsal shots of my childhood
       massed in mirage before me.
Of course I was child
And my first swallow of the liquor of battle bleeding
       black air dying and demon noise
Made me wild.

It was kinder than that, though, and I showed like a
       banner my kindness.
I loved. And a man will guard when he loves.
Their white-gowned democracy was my fair lady.
With her knife lying cold, straight, in the softness of her
       sweet-flowing sleeve.
But for the sake of the dear smiling mouth and the
       stuttered promise I toyed with my life.
I threw back! — I would not remember
Entirely the knife.

Still — am I good enough to die for them, is my blood
       bright enough to be spilled,
Was my constant back-question — are they clear
On this? Or do I intrude even now?

Am I clean enough to kill for them, do they
    wish me to kill
For them or is my place while death licks his lips and
    strides to them
In the galley still?

(In a southern city a white man said
Indeed, I'd rather be dead;
Indeed, I'd rather be shot in the head
Or ridden to waste on the back of a flood
Than saved by the drop of a black man's blood.)

Naturally, the important thing is, I helped to save them,
    them and a part of their democracy.
Even if I had to kick their law into their teeth in order
    to do that for them.
And I am feeling well and settled in myself because I
    believe it was a good job,
Despite this possible horror: that they might prefer the
Preservation of their law in all its sick dignity and their
    knives
To the continuation of their creed
And their lives.

I LOVE THOSE LITTLE BOOTHS
AT BENVENUTI'S

They get to Benvenuti's. There are booths
To hide in while observing tropical truths
About this — dusky folk, so clamorous!
So colorfully incorrect,

So amorous,
So flatly brave!
Boothed-in, one can detect,
Dissect.

One knows and scarcely knows what to expect.

What antics, knives, what lurching dirt; what ditty —
Dirty, rich, carmine, hot, not bottled up,
Straining in sexual soprano, cut
And praying in the bass, partial, unpretty.

They sit, sup,
(Whose friends, if not themselves, arrange
To rent in Venice "a very large cabana,
Small palace," and eat mostly what is strange.)
They sit, they settle; presently are met
By the light heat, the lazy upward whine
And lazy croaky downward drawl of "Tanya."
And their interiors sweat.
They lean back in the half-light, stab their stares
At: walls, panels of imitation oak
With would-be marbly look; linoleum squares
Of dusty rose and brown with little white splashes,
White curls; a vendor tidily encased;
Young yellow waiter moving with straight haste,
Old oaken waiter, lolling and amused;
Some paper napkins in a water glass;
Table, initialed, rubbed as a desk in school.

They stare. They tire. They feel refused,
Feel overwhelmed by subtle treasons!
Nobody here will take the part of jester.

The absolute stutters, and the rationale
Stoops off in astonishment.
But not gaily
And not with their consent.

They play "They All Say I'm The Biggest Fool"
And "Voo Me On The Vot Nay" and "New Lester
Leaps In" and "For Sentimental Reasons."

But how shall they tell people they have been
Out Bronzeville way? For all the nickels in
Have not bought savagery or defined a "folk."

The colored people will not "clown."

The colored people arrive, sit firmly down,
Eat their Express Spaghetti, their T-bone steak,
Handling their steel and crockery with no clatter,
Laugh punily, rise, go firmly out of the door.

A MAN OF THE MIDDLE CLASS

I'm what has gone out blithely and with noise
Returning! I'm what rushed around to pare
Down rind, to find fruit frozen under there.

I am bedraggled, with sundry dusts to be shed;
Trailing desperate tarnished tassels. These strident Aprils
With terrifying polkas and Bugle Calls
Confound me.

— Although I've risen! and my back is bold.
My tongue is brainy, choosing from among
Care, rage, surprise, despair, and choosing care.
I'm semi-splendid within what I've defended.

Yet, there I totter, there limp laxly. My
Uncomely trudge
To plateau That and platitudinous Plateau
Whichever is no darling to my grudge-
Choked industry or usual alcohol.

I've roses to guard
In the architectural prettiness of my yard.
(But there are no paths remarkable for wide
Believable welcomes.)

I have loved directions.
I have loved orders and an iron to stride, I,
Whose hands are papers now,
Fit only for tossing in this outrageous air.

Not God nor grace nor candy balls
Will get me everything different and the same!

My wife has canvas walls.

My wife never quite forgets to put flowers in vases,
Bizarre prints in the most unusual places,
Give teas for poets, wear odoriferous furs.
An awful blooming is hers.

I've antique firearms. Blackamoors. Chinese
Rugs. Ivories.
Bronzes. Everything I Wanted.
But have I answers? Oh methinks

I've answers such as have
The executives I copied long ago,
The ones who, forfeiting Vicks salve,
Prayer book and Mother, shot themselves last Sunday.
All forsaking
All that was theirs but for their money's taking.

I've answers such as Giants used to know.
There's a Giant who'll jump next Monday; all forsaking
Wives, safes and solitaire
And the elegant statue standing at the foot of the stair.

THE SUNDAYS OF
SATIN-LEGS SMITH

Inamoratas, with an approbation,
Bestowed his title. Blessed his inclination.

He wakes, unwinds, elaborately: a cat
Tawny, reluctant, royal. He is fat
And fine this morning. Definite. Reimbursed.

He waits a moment, he designs his reign,
That no performance may be plain or vain.
Then rises in a clear delirium.

He sheds, with his pajamas, shabby days.
And his desertedness, his intricate fear, the
Postponed resentments and the prim precautions.

Now, at his bath, would you deny him lavender
Or take away the power of his pine?
What smelly substitute, heady as wine,
Would you provide? Life must be aromatic.
There must be scent, somehow there must be some.
Would you have flowers in his life? suggest
Asters? a Really Good geranium?
A white carnation? Would you prescribe a Show
With the cold lilies, formal chrysanthemum
Magnificence, poinsettias, and emphatic
Red of prize roses? might his happiest
Alternative (you muse) be, after all,
A bit of gentle garden in the best
Of taste and straight tradition? Maybe so.
But you forget, or did you ever know,
His heritage of cabbage and pigtails,
Old intimacy with alleys, garbage pails,
Down in the deep (but always beautiful) South
Where roses blush their blithest (it is said)
And sweet magnolias put Chanel to shame.

No! He has not a flower to his name.
Except a feather one, for his lapel.
Apart from that, if he should think of flowers
It is in terms of dandelions or death.
Ah, there is little hope. You might as well —
Unless you care to set the world a-boil
And do a lot of equalizing things,
Remove a little ermine, say, from kings,
Shake hands with paupers and appoint them men,
For instance — certainly you might as well
Leave him his lotion, lavender and oil.

Let us proceed. Let us inspect, together
With his meticulous and serious love,
The innards of this closet. Which is a vault
Whose glory is not diamonds, not pearls,
Not silver plate with just enough dull shine.
But wonder-suits in yellow and in wine,
Sarcastic green and zebra-striped cobalt.
With shoulder padding that is wide
And cocky and determined as his pride;
Ballooning pants that taper off to ends
Scheduled to choke precisely.
                                        Here are hats
Like bright umbrellas; and hysterical ties
Like narrow banners for some gathering war.

People are so in need, in need of help.
People want so much that they do not know.

Below the tinkling trade of little coins
The gold impulse not possible to show
Or spend. Promise piled over and betrayed.

These kneaded limbs receive the kiss of silk.
Then they receive the brave and beautiful
Embrace of some of that equivocal wool.
He looks into his mirror, loves himself —
The neat curve here; the angularity
That is appropriate at just its place;
The technique of a variegated grace.

Here is all his sculpture and his art
And all his architectural design.
Perhaps you would prefer to this a fine
Value of marble, complicated stone.

Would have him think with horror of baroque,
Rococo. You forget and you forget.

He dances down the hotel steps that keep
Remnants of last night's high life and distress.
As spat-out purchased kisses and spilled beer.
He swallows sunshine with a secret yelp.
Passes to coffee and a roll or two.
Has breakfasted.
                    Out. Sounds about him smear,
Become a unit. He hears and does not hear
The alarm clock meddling in somebody's sleep;
Children's governed Sunday happiness;
The dry tone of a plane; a woman's oath;
Consumption's spiritless expectoration;
An indignant robin's resolute donation
Pinching a track through apathy and din;
Restaurant vendors weeping; and the L
That comes on like a slightly horrible thought.

Pictures, too, as usual, are blurred.
He sees and does not see the broken windows
Hiding their shame with newsprint; little girl
With ribbons decking wornness, little boy
Wearing trousers with the decentest patch,
To honor Sunday; women on their way
From "service," temperate holiness arranged
Ably on asking faces; men estranged
From music and from wonder and from joy
But far familiar with the guiding awe
Of foodlessness.
                    He loiters.
                              Restaurant vendors

Weep, or out of them rolls a restless glee.
The Lonesome Blues, the Long-lost Blues, I Want A
Big Fat Mama. Down these sore avenues
Comes no Saint-Saëns, no piquant elusive Grieg,
And not Tschaikovsky's wayward eloquence
And not the shapely tender drift of Brahms.
But could he love them? Since a man must bring
To music what his mother spanked him for
When he was two: bits of forgotten hate,
Devotion: whether or not his mattress hurts:
The little dream his father humored: the thing
His sister did for money: what he ate
For breakfast — and for dinner twenty years
Ago last autumn: all his skipped desserts.

The pasts of his ancestors lean against
Him. Crowd him. Fog out his identity.
Hundreds of hungers mingle with his own,
Hundreds of voices advise so dexterously
He quite considers his reactions his,
Judges he walks most powerfully alone,
That everything is — simply what it is.

But movie-time approaches, time to boo
The hero's kiss, and boo the heroine
Whose ivory and yellow it is sin
For his eye to eat of. The Mickey Mouse,
However, is for everyone in the house.

Squires his lady to dinner at Joe's Eats.
His lady alters as to leg and eye,
Thickness and height, such minor points as these,
From Sunday to Sunday. But no matter what

Her name or body positively she's
In Queen Lace stockings with ambitious heels
That strain to kiss the calves, and vivid shoes
Frontless and backless, Chinese fingernails,
Earrings, three layers of lipstick, intense hat
Dripping with the most voluble of veils.
Her affable extremes are like sweet bombs
About him, whom no middle grace or good
Could gratify. He had no education
In quiet arts of compromise. He would
Not understand your counsels on control, nor
Thank you for your late trouble.
                                        At Joe's Eats
You get your fish or chicken on meat platters.
With coleslaw, macaroni, candied sweets,
Coffee and apple pie. You go out full.
(The end is — isn't it? — all that really matters.)

        And even and intrepid come
        The tender boots of night to home.

        Her body is like new brown bread
        Under the Woolworth mignonette.

        Her body is a honey bowl
        Whose waiting honey is deep and hot.
        Her body is like summer earth,
        Receptive, soft, and absolute . . .

PAUL CARROLL *grew up in Chicago and received his M.A. in English from the University of Chicago in 1952. He served as poetry editor of* Chicago Review *from 1957-59 and founded and edited* Big Table, *a magazine associated with the Beat movement, 1959-61. He edited and introduced* The Edward Dahlberg Reader. *His poems have appeared in many periodicals, including* The Nation, Evergreen Review, The New Yorker, Poetry Magazine, Chicago Review, *and* Choice. *Currently he teaches in the Writers Workshop at the University of Iowa.*

ODE OF THE ANGELS OF CHICAGO WHO MOVE PERPETUALLY TOWARDS THE DAYSPRING OF THEIR YOUTH

To James Dickey, John Logan, and James Wright, and to my students in the poetry workshop at The University of Iowa during the second semester of 1966.

I

All over Chicago, Jim, the angels are making love.
Over there on Lakeview Avenue
Nearby the Zoo,
The psychiatrist, caressing, kissing,

Makes Sunday morning love with his delighted wife.
Beneath this bone-chipping,
Bone-dry Brueghelean sky,
Mobs of kids careen on Christmas sleds

Down the highest hill in Lincoln Park, their cries
The sounds of the original animals;
Their faces wool ski masks,
Barbaric, bright,

Flash by, like, abruptly,
In the middle of a confusing dream, a hand
In traffic cop's big orange glove
Begins to write a poem.

Remember, Jim, that winter noon we goof-
ed around this Zoo? That grey timber wolf
            moving with rage
        and the dignity of an old devil
            around its cage
        containing a tiny concrete hill,
moved you to wonder: "Isn't it marvellous
that we're allowed to live in the same universe
        with such a splendid beast!"
            You made a feast
        of words. But I was fascinated
            by how the grated
shadows of the wolf made an artificial night
in the middle of the raw, abundant haze of light.
            Now, in the middle
        of my 39th year, I yell
            to you, Jim, and John
        and you, Jim Wright: Here in the sun
I know how durable the feel of human joy —
the roots of human joy which nothing can destroy.

II

Another park glitters at the margin of my memory
I rushed twenty blocks to find, frantic
in the chill spring of 1953,
John, two months before we met by accident
one midnight in South Bend —
two poets in their twenties frightened by
the skeletons
of words.
And I found that you believed in angels too.

Shellacked by oil and scum from the Chrysler factory
the river I remember
carrying the light along it
and away.
Inexplicably my veins filling with bright air. Dusk
floating through the concrete bridge (pieces
of park
vanishing) cracked roots of trees and cut
open again
the need for something green
to grasp.
And I knew I had come to bring blood for the angel.
But I wanted to walk
as if sunlight weren't splintering in the river —
as if dusk were
more than cold
inside my wrists.
I became light, light flowing in the river. Foot
suddenly caught
in roots more primitive than any twilight.
My hand of fury

and dead words — I stood
cursing roots, trees, the ghosts of the birds,
that green moon —
cursed bridge and blood and flood of the river
not able to cover the wound —
O the angel singing
(a bird spread hard wings inside the bright nimbus)
of the humiliation
of encroaching bone.

III

My big body, Jim, feels filled with poems today.
The long shadows of the Chicago afternoon
Are the silos of tomorrow.
I want to live as if each day
Were the final poem I will ever write.
There is another night
And day inside of us;
Other trees;
And the old, reliable sewingmachines
Of love;
And the birds of pure desire.
And I sometimes have an intimation that
There is another ocean too, eternal, containing
The incandescence and the shadows
Of a multitude
Of the holy wasps —
An ocean from whom we have emerged and to whom we
shall return
In the painful ecstasy
Of the several births
We are.

IV

I feel so goddamn good today I try
the old corkscrew windup of Leroy (Tarzan) Parmalee
    pitching a snowball at a tree.
When I meet my first class in the poetry workshop at the
University of Iowa next month,
I want to rush into the room like Groucho Marx —
    his crouching zany zip
        (like Yogi Berra roller skating into New Year's
        Eve) —
puffing on his outsized stogie
        as he circles ritzy Mable Norman in *A Day at the*
        Races,
saying: "So you kids want to learn about poetry, eh?
Well, a poem can wear galoshes too. Or sit,
        doing the daily crossword puzzle on the bus.

A poem can be the melancholy
hardon
of an angel.
            Or a way to box
            desire in and
            shut it out
            for good.
                Or exorcise the bees
                about the heart.

A poem can also be (circle one of the following three):

(1) The girdle of the grandmother of Hugh Hefner
(2) The surprisingly low fare on the meters of the *Yellow*
    taxicabs of purgatory
(3) The chameleons of our feelings (they seldom sleep)
(4) None of the above

Or a poem can take as text
Hobbes' observation that
the life of humankind (in
a state of nature, Ginsberg) is
solitary,
poor,
nasty,
brutish
and short.

Or to put the question in another way:
Do our emotions also flourish best
in a country with a strong and prudent constitution
      and laws formulated by adult intelligence?
Or does Thoreau's incisive acid statement win the day:
      "Our manners have been corrupted by
      communication with the saints," confessing:
"As I came home through the woods
with my string of fish,
trailing my pole, it
now being quite dark, I caught
a glimpse
of a woodchuck
stealing across my path,
and felt a strange thrill
of savage delight, and was sorely tempted to seize and
devour him raw;
not that I was hungry then
except for the wildness which he represented."

A poem can also be a way of digging that everything is
true:
for example, take
that accidental encounter

on the 1890 operating table
between a "sewing machine" and an umbrella;
or the things that men have died for:
    (a) Better wages
    (b) Liberty
    (c) The Arian Heresy
    (d) The Third Reich of the 1000 years
    (e) Love. Alcohol. Poetry
    (f) The Oedipus Complex
    (g) Or like Li Po trying to embrace "a moon/In
        the Yellow River"
    (h) Or like Socrates dying because of his lust for
        immortality in the memory and talk of men.

A poem is like the truth of the dreams of the baboons;
and like any successful marriage
   its skin and bones of style
are more than half of what it's all about.

        But a poem
        probably couldn't be about (unless
        you write damn well)

'the beautiful Oscar Meyer billboard Hog —'

the beautiful Oscar Meyer billboard Hog —

ing the corner of Michigan and Chestnut Street
with its reappearing icons of Pop Art:
the Gargantuan but loving hand of Granny
fondling a package of Canadian bacon; the heart
of succulent and plump red hots — "Treat

the entire family every Sunday" —

inside the hot dog heart the kids and dog

and Daddy too; and then the Xmas goose
all alone upon a checker cloth, like Moose
Salters whiffing with the bases loaded in
the ninth, big as the big protest from the behind
of Martin Luther (Cf.: Erikson,

Erik H.: *Young Man Luther*. His book's fun.)
            (The riff
            that you've just heard
            was pretty cornball, wasn't it? Take
            my word for it:
            Stay away from Pop.)

On the other hand,
a poem can be about Severn Darden being
the one and only entry under "Philosopher"
        in the pages of the *Yellow Book;*
or be about the ballet
or the Monkey Frug Watusi Mashed Potatoes Swim or
Jerk or Twist
        performed by certain Caribbean fish;
or about the six spectacular architectural proofs for God's
existence
mapped out by St Thomas Aquinas in his intellect
        in which fresh grass grew
        and a young ox flew gracefully by in the sky forever.
A poem can be nasty too —
like the bitterly uncomfortable second day
        of subzero weather in Chicago.
Or like truth.

Or be about the ambiguity of the icons of our memory.

    Or the telegrams
    which float from the unconscious
  to be translated by everyday acts of prose
  in our living rooms and kitchens
and in the empty bedroom which waits to turn into a
    nursery.

A poem can even be about the old secrets of the snow.

    Or the tractors of the psychoanalysts.
Every poem is probably a journey
but the destination's frequently ambiguous;
the map is your heart's fetishes,
its obscure gestures, primitive needs and postures;
to give them tongue it helps to use your head
and let your imagination go for broke:
but only in the absolute sense that Yeats implied
when he remarked on Donne:
"The intricacy and subtleties of Donne's imagination
are the length and depths of the furrow
made by his passion.
Donne's pedantry and (his) obscenity —
the rock and loam of his Eden —
but make me the more certain that
one who is but a man like all of us
has seen God."
    (I want to go home and make a baby with my wife.)
Most of all,
I want to recommend the possibility
of what the great Neruda calls
    "impure" poetry —

the art that can delineate
"the confused impurity of the human condition";
an art impure as the clothing that we wear;
or as impure as the daily miracle which is our body,
stained
      by soup and promises
      and the shame of our behavior,
our body electric with the shocks
of the occasional beautiful encounters with each other;
an impure poetry containing real telephone numbers
(321-7200. Encyclopaedia Britannica. Good morning.)
and Anita Eckberg's breasts of glass,
Christ in his skin, breathing, for two hours one afternoon
in a bedroom in an apartment at 6719 South Ridgeland
Avenue, Chicago,
and the X-rays of the skeletons of taxes;
that is, a poetry as big as the proverbial barn door
     always open to admit
the whole heartbreaking carnival of the unconscious
     and also my Aunt Josephine;
a poetry which will never end until
those two long-legged airline stewardesses, exuding
the corny but abundant beauty of the Middlewest,
     turn into angels too
        (Ladies and Gentlemen,
   we'll arrive in Iowa City in approximately
   15 minutes.
The temperature there is 16 degrees.
   We hope you've enjoyed your flight on *Ozark*).
Outside my window
the propellor manufactures a multitude of rainbows
     out of sun and steel.

And (I hope
that you're still with me: Take
comfort in the fact
that you can rack up 6 full credit hours in this course)
        a poem can also be about the fact
                that you've an itch to write a poem
which is itself
the lovely, invisible poem of the air."

R. R. CUSCADEN *was born in Highland Park,
Illinois, and has lived his entire life in the state (pres-
ently in Geneva). During the day he is editor of the
industrial publication* Paperboard Packaging; *at night
he edits the poetry* little Midwest, *which he founded
in 1960. In 1953 he founded* Mainstream, *which in 1958
became* Odyssey, *and while studying at Roosevelt
University he founded and edited* Vigil (1959). *Two
chapbooks of his poetry have been published — Poem
For a Ten Pound Sailfish and Ups & Downs of a Third
Baseman. He is represented in anthologies, including
the* Borestone Mountain Best Poems of 1964, *and has
appeared in many periodicals, including* Saturday,
Chicago, Minnesota, San Francisco, North American,
Northwest *reviews,* Beloit Poetry Journal, *and* December.

CARSHOPS AT CENTRALIA

There are men who have worked among all
This steel for fifty years. When I shake
Their hands I am touching the railroad.

When they were young and their youth
Made the old men smile, they thought:
I shall try this out; I can always leave.

Now they know they will never leave.
Their wives are dead, their sons are gone.
The change of seasons is strange to them.

When I speak to them they do not hear.
There is too much lost and forgotten,
Too many years, here, at Centralia, Illinois.

FREEPORT

There was something nagging me about Freeport.
All day up the old main line from Centralia
Some memory scratched away and wanted out.
But whatever it was — a girl, a baseball game,
A poem — was in too deep. I gave it up.

That night, standing in the shower, six bottles
Of beer and a rare steak shifting uneasily
In my belly, I remembered all about Freeport:
A girl, a baseball game, a poem — the three
Together, on a warm afternoon in Freeport.

A PASSING

On the highway to Decatur
The automobile is overtaken,
Passed by a freight train.

The boxcars seem to pass forever.

I am caught up in the strange excitement
Of moving things, the clash and rattle
Of metal.

Yes, that is it, that is it, I say over and over.

But you are not by my side.
There is only a sleeping stranger,
Crouched low in the thicket of her black hair.

SUMMER STORM

My giant, aged (and leaning) Cottonwood tree,
Splendidly singular in a forest of backyards,
Is filling the air with a storm of white tufts.
Democratically, the wind is distributing
These melt-less snowflakes into everyone's yard.
We are forgetting no one. And no one seems grateful.
My neighbor on the left has been out to rake
Three times this afternoon, and will not speak;
My neighbor on the right stands in his yard
(A white, fluttering crown on his head)
And offers the loan of a power saw.

Back and forth through this glorious downpour
Fly multitudes of birds. Most of them
Have nests in the garage (I never remember
To close the door). A humanist even in
Avian circles, I nod at their coming and going —
Though they whiten the roof of my car.

Trying to finish a poem in the midst
Of all this uproar, I dream of buying
An old caboose, setting it under my
Cottonwood, writing within its wooden quiet
Before the storm of years comes to an end.

A POEM FOR EMILY

On certain windless nights, the diesels
Drift down through the hills of northern
Iowa without making a single sound.

There is only the sense of something being
There. As when one wakes at night, and
Senses his wife sleeping at his side.

Or, as now, when told of the birth of
A friend's first child: a sense of someone
Being there: named, but unseen, unknown.

EDWARD HOPPER'S "HOUSE BY THE TRACKS"

It is, I suppose, Victorian.
But, Early? Mid? Late? Who knows?
Another great gap in my meager knowledge.
Some days, I barely know my name.
But those windows!
Open wounds across the body of a century.
I see myself crouched behind that fourth-floor
Window, running a bony finger along
The beaded panes. It is all a part of waiting;
But not (really) expecting anything to
Come rolling by on those rusty tracks.

OLD DAVENPORT DAYS

for Shirley Reay

Trainmen, ancient, in their cups, sliding
Coins across the polished and sweating
Wood of the bar, wiping gnarled hands
Clean of pigs' feet against Oshkosh overalls,
Can tell of love, here, in old Davenport.

There are elm-shadowed grandmothers who
Remember (fondly) what they used to do
With trainmen roaring off the Rock Island.
Nights when no one living seems that kind
Come often now, here, in old Davenport.

HOAR-FROST, STATION SMOKE, RUSTY TRACKS

What we wait for is often late.
Or not coming at all.

Like now, alone with hoar-frost,
Station smoke, and rusty tracks.

I know of no one else waiting for
Express trains on forgotten branch lines.

There are those who will know what I mean.

SOLD

After many long months on the market,
The *For Sale* sign flaking paint,
My house is finally sold.
Poor wallflower of a buy,
No one loved you but the basement poet.
When the wind blew west
The paint factory sent my wife
Into a flurry of window-shutting;
The children somehow never found
The friends they impossibly imagined.
But my radishes prospered
In that southside, White Sox air,
And my single tree, a Cottonwood,
Ruled a forest of backyards.

Now, it is hard to recall
The sounds and passing of the
Illinois Central freight trains,
And there is no ground I can call my own.

WHEAT

Musty with love, we are gathered up
By the wind and the wheat we lie in.
The sun drives the color of gold
Into our silent, white bodies.
Birds from ancient clouds
Slip across my eyes;
Miles and miles away,

A tractor burrows up and down
The summer.
Closeby, the *Overland* whistles
Its way through the thick wheat,
Flattens acres and acres of wheat
With its passing.
A shower of cinders
Draws you to me once again.

BRUCE CUTLER, *whose first collection of poems*
The Year of the Green Wave *was published in 1960
with an introduction by Karl Shapiro, teaches English
at the University of Wichita. A native of Illinois, he
holds degrees from the University of Iowa (A.B., 1951)
and Kansas State University (A.M., 1957). He served
four years with the American Friends Service Com-
mittee, mostly in Latin America, and spent a year in
Naples as a Fulbright fellow. In 1962 he brought out*
A West Wind Rises *and in 1964* Sun City *(sixteen poems
and a translation).*

WHERE WE ARE

Iron bands
and squared-off trunks, and tree-
spines rising either side,
hung again in iron
and in copper with the ring
of glass glinting beneath,
and beyond, a scam

of green November wheat
all caulked with snow
gunned from the great galena sky:

at a wye, standing by a wooden coach
that geysers steam behind,
capitals above its windows
softening into drift,
looking along this spur
to where
the handswitch heart
shudders in winds from both Dakotas,
waiting for the *Eagle, Zephyr,*
Rocket, Flyer, Chief:

sheep-lined with a black
Detroit around my ears, the brakeman
gauntleted and gazing down the track
for what we do not see or hear, yet know
is there:
and here just out of Harper, Geuda Springs,
Holyrood and Hitschman,
heading for Geneseo, Englewood,
Concordia or Pratt,
throwing our switches, backing, dropping,
picking up two hundred miles in pieces
in the steel of reefers, hoppers, flats,

we wait, and we are cold,
and there is nothing down our track but pieces,
humps and elevators, dehydrators, dumps,
snowfence pickets and battened sheds,

two hundred miles of pieces gained
a tie, a rail, a section at a time,
a message sent on insulators
pole by pole, dit by dot —
a run a day of pieces gathered up
along this seam of plains
where we stand in roaring steam and snow,
waiting for you.

SUN CITY

Three thousand days of Kansas sun,
and it comes on again: the six o'clock
and steel perimeter
upturns beyond the sums and squares
of window sash, and runs
along the asphalt shingles
of a roof curling
into coral conflagration,
the air between us burning,
burning into day.

You sleep. I open inward,
extend my waking fingers
out of the nests of night.
Away, a diesel thrums
as deep and quiet as a heart.
A heart. Two hearts,
bedded on a daybreak spur at head
of track, where the Kansas sun comes on,
comes on like a rising of the blood,
of lids and eyes, comes on.

I feel my arms extend through walls,
through glass and the penny smell of soap,
through the green of cottonwoods
and the snow of seed and the aphid rain,
through dust that devils at the roots
and blows and blackjacks in the bottoms,
where the tenth, the heaviest hand of summer
drives in stakes of light,
the air between us burning,
burning into day.

We touch. You are my rambler rose,
my slumbering rambler
clambering the claybanks of my flesh,
greening the face of dust,
raising the ghost of water to the leaf,
to the morningstars that open, close,
searching the face of sun
as it comes on,
comes on like a rising of the blood,
of lids and eyes, comes on.

A bell. The diesel hacks.
A brakeman winds his flare.
The tissue of the dawn is torn
as couplings yank and hammer.
Ahead lie Attica, Belvidere.
Forest City. Sharon.
Ahead like the rising of the blood,
of lids and eyes, the air between us burning,
at end of track there lies
the city of the sun.

THE FIRES OF LIFE

The fires of life burn only in a drop
of water. A dry root or tongue that tastes
of that incredible flame will never stop
its drinking till the flame is flesh and wastes
no nutrient power. We'd rule with water if
our souls knew the metabolism of rain —
what giants our hearts would be! Pressures that cliff
the Colorado limestone beds and chain-
diastrophy that rocks mountains awake
are vulnerable to a drop, that turned to ice,
can rive a million years and tons and break
systems into ships' ballast. But we feed
a proud appetite, and water twice
confounds us, gathering in the sun for seed.

OX DRIVER

Les Très Riches Heures du Duc de Berry

October. Sows and boars crash in the leaves
of maple groves. Simmering oak
branches, the color of blood, soak
up strength from a dying sun. Heaves
have broken the horse's wind
and frost covers his watering trough: a cracked
oven burns the meat and gives our wine a sacked
taste. My hands so cold they feel skinned —
still, the ox plows pastern-deep, opening neat
furrows to broadcast winter wheat.

FROM A NATURALIST'S NOTEBOOK: SMOKE

Beyond the twirling keys of sycamores
and coil of anaconda hills,
smoke interrogates
a washed West Kansas sky.
As keen as cold
that tumbleweeds through trees,
white and icarian in a weight
of air, it soon convolves
and rises into space.

Not even a thrush
forgets itself to music
the way that silent smoke
involves itself in air.
Earth's own amplexity,
fat and fleshed and veined,
boned, limbed and skinned,
it grows somehow immune
to faltering or falling.

Evolving in a helicline
smoke commits itself
to constant reformation,
sometimes by drift of wind,
by sunlight and shade, humidity
and heat: existing
sometimes *no* and sometimes *yes*,
lost in a soul of sky,
inessential and complete.

THE CIMARRON

ex. Jrnl. Max. Greene, 1851

I left the Rockies by the Ratone gate,
descending long detrital avenues
through porticoes of columnar quartz,
then walked surefooted in the sands that rose
at a green chatauqua of cedars
slumbering beside attendant springs.
I camped, and gazed eastward across a land
the diastrophic hand of God had thrown
unjumbled in the wake of mountain chains:
a burned-out tabernacle of a plain,
its dry dimensions dazzling in the motes
of lead glass mirrors in the sky.

But I set forth from those cool embrasures
across the pages of a burning book
and wrote myself discoverer
of winds, whose undertow soon drowned my trail
and scabbed the corners of my eyes and mouth.
Day after day I saw no sign of life,
no mound, not even smoke. There was no refuge
in the nights: beneath incendiary blasts
of stars, I heard familiar voices, the chink
of harness, hymns and reels, laughter and the like.
But in the steel engraving of the dawn,
all was gone except the wind, except the wind.

After I bore a hundred miles to east
I came upon cold emigrant camps.
I guessed they'd headed for the Cimarron
and water, for ruts of wagons ran

a gauntlet between some bolts of crinoline,
a clavichord, a grandfather's clock
high on the horizon, chiming like a church;
then oxen picked to gristle; half
a wagon with a hundredweight of flour;
farther on, a cart and bags of pemmican;
then some gravemounds, a wheelbarrow smashed.
A boot. And two days beyond, the Cimarron.

It tore the prairie with a soundless stream
of air, as crystalline as quartz,
its banks pocked with hollows, bare of brush.
Descending, I saw projecting bluffs
nodular with clay, that looked like forts
the Sioux had burned. I signed my footprints
into the bed broken only by y's
of dry arroyos pouring in their loads
of oven air. And at daysend, I found
a saline spring, with a lone euphorbia
silver-veined and green as a mirage.
But not a track or tracing of a man.

Sighting along those shimmering streams of air
it seemed the falling sun had pulled me down
into the valleys of Cimmeria
and I was forced to meditate upon
portals of a last reality
that one man in his self-confidence had passed
and merciful divinity had slain
and metamorphosed — into a plant that spread
pretensions of a shade around its springs.
Nearby, beneath a boulder, I heard
a hiss insinuating ways
of entering in that myth. But I turned around.

LETTER FROM FORT SCOTT

October: having left the Platte,
we crosstracked geese and mallard.
They are long since gone, and we
are the hunted of this rawboned air,
sojourning in a dun
and sumac-ridden surf of grass that rolls
in slow insinuations on the edge
of flathead hills, curving out of eyeshot.
Even the sun has seemed to move
outward in space, leaving the sky
weak-winded in its vacuum,
so silent that our rowels chink
like circus tambourines from ridge to ridge.

At night, the sky dimensions into stars
and banks of Northern Lights
arch in lurid coruscations East to West,
blue to green to violet, crimson fires
flashing, darting up, or streaming across
the skulls of prehistoric hills,
men and mules and dogs' eyes,
falling exhausted in their force,
leaving us little more obscured
even suspecting that we heard them fall:
each of us alone, each of flesh
on which such forces play
as scribble over heaven, spattering stars.

THE LANGUAGE OF YES

Our fifth year. And even the heart's highplain
is wound with westering columns of our love,
our body's sod parabled with grain,
mind's aspens opened to mercies of the dove.
We grow in leaf-green mansions toward the sun
and drive our roots with wild-plum discipline;
so colonized, the sky-high West we've won
will outweather ice and alkaline.
And there is a tongue to our frontier
you hear on hummingbirds and talltale youth,
on old-time homesteads where hills confess
the joyful noises of a heyday here,
of love and love for life and living truth,
and all the lessons of that language, yes.

FREDERICK ECKMAN, *who was born in Continental, Ohio, did his doctoral thesis at Ohio State on* The Language of American Poetry, 1900-1910. *As an undergraduate he served on the staff of* Cronos, *and in 1948, along with Richard Emerson, founded* Golden Goose, *which published as one of its chapbooks* The Pink Church *by William Carlos Williams. He has been a teacher since 1949, and presently teaches creative writing at Bowling Green University. His poems have appeared in a variety of magazines, and he has published a study of contemporary American poetry,* Cobras and Cockle Shells, *and several volumes of verse:* XXV Poems, The Exile, Hot & Cold: Running, *and* The Epistemology of Loss.

TO SHERWOOD ANDERSON,
IN HEAVEN

Last September, on the road to Sandusky,
I counted blackbirds, flocks of them,
whistling & flapping in the harvest fields
under that gold Indian-summer sun which you
must still remember, twenty years now in Heaven.
My father, driving the car, talked of crops
& weather, keeping his eye on the white line.
He did not appear to notice the blackbirds.
But then he is seventy years old; his eyes
turn mostly backward: into a past that you,
Sherwood, gave a kind of gloomy immortality.

I disturb my father; he does not understand
who or what I am: a happy lunatic, a poet,
a bear-like man with a beard, a cloud-watcher,
a shameless sensualist: eating, drinking, talking,
reading, laughing, cursing, weeping, smoking — all
too much; lover of flowers & small children,
an eye for the women, a stylist, a tragic clown,
incurable romancer from my earliest days.
My father — austere, silent, ascetic: almost
a Roman — must wonder where I came from:
surely not, he thinks, from these lean loins!

So, anyway, when we reached Fremont, we found
the highway under construction: yes, Sherwood,
they are still at it up there — progress, progress.
"We'll have to detour through Clyde," Father said.
Pretending not to remember, I asked him what kind

of town Clyde was. "Oh, a nice little place,"
he said. Somehow I was hoping he'd add, "Sherwood
Anderson used to live there." Then we could have
talked about you all the way into Sandusky.
But he didn't, so I pulled my guitar out of
the back seat & played some Mexican songs
while the blackbirds swooped & ascended
over the harvest fields, & while my father
watched the white highway line into Clyde.

Damn it, Sherwood, this is *my* country too!
You & my father cannot have it all. Like you,
I know the look of ponds at sunset on the edges
of small Ohio towns; county fairs are more real
to me than art galleries or seminar rooms; I too
have smoked cornsilk in cool dark barns; I have been
a poor boy with a newspaper route; I have heard
the old veterans, spitting & droning around
a pot-bellied stove in the general store; I too
had a gentle weary mother who died young.
Let me in, Sherwood! Let me in, Father!
All three of us have whooped drunkenly in village streets
through the sexual explosion of Ohio spring. Let me in!

We went fishing, my father & I, in Sandusky Bay.
It's a fine place, Sherwood, as you must recall;
but not as quiet & rural as when you & Doc Reefy
sat there on summer afternoons. There are rows
of cottages now, filling stations & a beer tavern
or two. The city people have found it: their harsh
voices & loud radios hang in the summer air. But
the fish are still there: bass & perch & sheephead.

If you go out into the bay with a boat, all the shore
noises fade away, & you can be alone with the lake
& the sun & the shoreline. I wanted to bring some beer,
but my father thinks I drink too much (I do), so
we took water instead. I think it made him happy
that I fished with him that afternoon. Suddenly,
coming back to shore, I wanted to weep for whatever
        it was
that my father & I had never shared. But of course
I didn't, & we drove back to Continental in the dark.

So I am sitting here, Sherwood, two seasons later,
in surroundings that you would recognize at once:
a shabby room in a strange city, far away from Clyde
or Sandusky or Continental. There are no harvest fields,
no blackbirds outside my window. I am thirty-five
years old: a shaggy man at a typewriter, half his life
behind him. I write poems, or try to. People in Ohio
think it a fantastic way of life, & I suppose it is.
Like you, I have no regrets for having abandoned
all those fine abstractions — marriage, success, prestige,
security — for the solid meat of things: words, trees,
women's lips, flowers; grime, leaky commodes,
        gas burners,
the cold asphalt of night streets. No, I am simply here:
a live man in the realest of all possible worlds.

But this was not what I started out to say.
What I want to know, Sherwood, if you can hear me,
sitting up there at some celestial trotting race,
or loafing in some heavenly harness shop or poolroom,

or doing whatever it is that saintly dead writers might
    find
to do in Heaven — what I'd like to know, Sherwood,
is who my father is. Are you my father? Is he my father?
Is God my father? Send me a message, Sherwood.

LONG DISTANCE

Now & then the connection is lost.
Bad conditions, they say: lines jammed up,

weather ugly, the terminal points
far distant in space or sorrow, time,

death, joy. Yet somehow the filament
holds — past whatever damage ice, flame,

wind, & the slow corrosion of habit
can offer. Words still run on the wire,

the friend at the other end is there:
he will answer when it rings again.

OLD MAN, PHANTOM DOG

In late autumn the hound,
gone now ten years, has come

— or so it seems to him,
sunk in a chair at dusk —

to scratch at the back door,
its whine a faint murmur

in the cold evening. Then
his mind will shift slowly

in its old skull-bone chair
to other falls fifty,

forty, thirty years now
torn out of time: black leaves

across the stubble-field
acres where love summered,

golden-ripe. The tall boys
were that grain: lost now too,

into towns, other worlds
— as if, like her, buried.

Can he, straining deafly,
hear the hound's tail thumping

on the doorsill? It is
cold, poor thing, dead these years.

If a wife sat there now
in the dark room, if she . . .

but who can struggle up
from the old chair to let

a ghostly hound grow warm
at the unlit stove? No,

let what is buried stay
safe in its warm burrow:

farmers rest in winter
— an axiom he has.

A LONG STORY

He is not hard to find:
hung up,

hooked on it, the most
willing victim

you'll ever see. What cruise
to Jamaica

would help him? Locomotives
thunder through

all his dreams. Let him
take ten trips

by airliner to exotic cities:
no cure there.

We must conclude, then
dear friends,

a hopeless case. He wants
no more

than all the world's love:
a small favor,

certainly, to one so free
with himself.

ALBA: WHOSE MUSE?

The cigarettes are all gone,
    a fact,
the coffee tastes like
    hot bilge.

O red eye, the mirror says:
    you fool
to fight all that darkness
    alone.

To which I agree. The air
    is stale,
the phonograph shut off
    in disgust.

If anything had been done:
    but no,
the blank paper lies there
    as before.

Outside, birds are raising
happy hell
through the blue intensities
of dawn.

She has not come to me
in weeks,
that slut. What can I do
but wait?

LIKE IN THE MOVIES

Life's little problems always
work out:

as, viz., the retired brakeman
next door —

paralyzed, but they give him
a pension.

Deserted, the young housewife
turns whore.

Or my friend who had cancer:
shot himself,

& why not? To these I
could add

numerous other consoling
examples.

She said: mix me a drink,
philosopher.

LOVE LIES A-BLEEDING

That they should quarrel
over garbage! Yet he *did*
fail to set it out, & now
it must fill the back porch
    with its putridness
for another three days.

There are no words
to reconcile this: a promise
forgotten, the passionate
    imbecility of love
    slashed open. Her loss
as well — who, grieving,
slams the cupboard doors
while he sulks on the couch,
    his heart drowning
in that mortal stench.

PAUL ENGLE, *born in Cedar Rapids, Iowa, attended Coe College, University of Iowa, Columbia University and, as a Rhodes Scholar, Oxford University.* Worn Earth, *his first volume, was the Yale University Press Prize book for 1932. His second volume,* American Song, *contains the poem "America Remembers," selected by* Poetry Magazine *to represent the Chicago Century of Progress. Succeeding volumes included* Break the Heart's Anger, Corn, West of Midnight, American Child, The Word of Love *and the novel* Always the Land. *His most recent volumes are* Poems in Praise *(1959) and* Woman

Unashamed *and Other Poems (1965). He was for six
years editor of the annual collection of O. Henry Prize
Stories. He has been on the faculty of University of Iowa
since 1937, and is the director of the Program in Creative
Writing there.*

from FOR THE IOWA DEAD

I

On this wall, in this town, in their own state
We name their individual names, to state
That they were not just group, crew, squad, alone,
But each one man, one mortal self, alone,
Who fought the brutal frenzy of his time,
Who touched with human hand this iron time.
We give to them, who died in every weather,
Grief like an old wound groaning with the weather.

They knew death as a family dog knows men,
By whistle, touch, familiar smell of men,
But still were cheerful, still could ask each morning,
What do you know for sure on a new morning?
Before death's final stammer in the throat
Knew love's live stammer in the breathing throat.

III

Morning Sun, Stone City, Boone, What Cheer:
In the hysteria of history
These names for home rang in the homesick ear,
With the warm sound of friend and family,
Of Iowa, where winter cracks your skull,

Where summer floats on fields, green river flowing,
Where autumn stains your hand with walnut hull,
Spring shakes the land with a loud gust of growing.

But their true season was the one of dying.
Summer, autumn, winter, spring all ran
Into one flaming moment, doomed plane flying,
Sinking ship, exploding shell, edged knife:
For home is not birthplace, but the place a man
Dares a way of death, to keep a way of life.

IV

Most of their life was simply, to make life:
The clover planted and the cattle bred,
Each year the wheat field ripped by the plough's clean
     knife,
The crust of earth cut like the crust of bread,
The fat hogs slopped, the ludicrous, loud hogs,
The skimmed milk saucered for the lazy cats,
The careful mating of the hunting dogs,
The oat bin plugged against the ravenous rats.

But then their life changed simply, to end lives:
The strange men killed less quickly than the brown
Beef steer by the sledge and the neat knives,
The child's hand begging but without an arm,
The cattle shelled in the defended farm,
The crazed cat shot for luck in the taken town.

VI

Some left green meadows for the greener ocean,
Left the low rising, falling of that land
For a more violent and reckless motion

No landscaped brain and body could withstand.
American bones beneath that brutal water
Move in the cold and restless bed of sea,
And have no dream of any woman's daughter
Warm in another bed that will never be.

Darker than earth is the sea-depth where they died,
A bitter grave in a salt and barren place
For those whose loam had made yield after yield.
Their chalk hand twitches but only with the tide.
Now is the lean and cropward-looking face
Gone from their skull like soil from a gullied field.

XII

Now in the fields ploughed by another's sweat
The native corn is tall. They will not go
To measure it with knee and thigh. But let
No pity cover them like sudden snow.
As Icarus in the fury of his fall
Rose through time to immortality,
So by their savage dying will they all
Live in this long war's monstrous memory.

But they would scrap that little fame to work
One hard hot day under the Kansas glare,
In Illinois, where the low hay mowers jerk,
In Iowa, where corn grows fat on the heat,
Or in the north Red River valley, where
The blond Norwegians harvest the blonder wheat.

XXII

Heart of the heartland, where the deep-plowed fields
Lie in huge harvest or the winter-wait,

Where human hope and food are the rich yields,
And nothing there to hate but mortal hate;
Marvelous, hearty, middle country, when
Winds of the world blow dark and full of warning,
Recall, in your great fullness, these dead men,
Homesick for one more live midwestern morning.

So, in a time of fear, have no dejection,
Remember these men on whose lives you stand.
Recall their name, face, human imperfection,
How their death gave life to this lucky land,
For memory is mortal resurrection,
Light as sun rising or a loving hand.

DAVE ETTER *was born in California but has lived
most of his life in the midwest. He graduated from the
University of Iowa in 1953 and has worked in Iowa,
Indiana, Missouri and Illinois, where he presently lives
(Geneva) and works (Chicago — in the editorial depart-
ment of Encyclopedia Britannica). His poems have ap-
peared in some fifty magazines, among them* Antioch
Review, Beloit Poetry Journal, Chicago Review, Choice,
Massachusetts Review, Prairie Schooner, *and* New
Mexico Quarterly. Go Read the River, *his first collection,
was published in 1966.*

THE HOMETOWN HERO
COMES HOME

This train, two Illinois counties late,
slips through jungles of corn and hot leaves,
and the blazing helmets of huge barns.

My head spins with too much beer and sun
and the mixed feelings of going home.

The coach window has melted my face.
I itch where a birthmark darkens my skin.

The Jewish woman who sits next to me
sheds tears for a son, dead in Viet Nam.
Her full lips are the color of crushed plums.
I want to go off with her to some lost
fishing village on the Mississippi
and be quiet among stones and small boats.

My fever breaks in the Galena hills.

It's too humid: no one will meet me.
And there are no brass bands in Dubuque.

WEDDING DAY

A blackbird sulks on the window sill
where I have carved a dozen hearts.

I am in love with gin and sleep.

Between the long shadows of red barns
a strange girl calls me to a marriage
under honeysuckle strung with bees.

High in this cupola bedroom
I drift off in a bell of leaves.

Soon, I will never be seen again.

WORDS FOR A FRIEND WHO WAS ACCIDENTALLY SHOT WHILE HUNTING PHEASANTS IN NORTHERN IOWA

. . . a day that has tasted the grief in our blood.
                                    PABLO NERUDA

Close weather wets the bricks on Hill Street.
Only one porch light fights the fog.

The midnight train to Mason City
is washed in rivers of the moon.

In the windy cave of a cornfield
your blood has dried on the bones of husks.

I have every right to love you.

INVITATION TO A YOUNG RIVER QUEEN

Purple fish leap for the sun.

The sun is my yellow hat
which I have tossed madly
into the bug-colored air.

I am quite beside myself with joy.

I love the fountains of grass
that spill over the river's edge.
I love worms and stones and bare toes.

You must come fishing with me.

You must come with your raintree sex,
your breasts of Easter eggs,
your thighs of taffy and moonflowers

And you must wear your yellow hat.

TWO DREAMS OF KANSAS

1
Forty-two grain elevators
have blown up
in Salina, Kansas.
I am buried in a loaf
of Sunbeam bread.

2
In a wheatfield
west of Hays
the fat thighs of a farm girl
are clamped around my loins.
I am dying of loneliness.

HOLLYHOCKS

Hollyhocks are swaying gently
under the blue branches of an elm.

I watch 82 freight cars
sink into the corn leaves
and drop over the rim of the prairie.

On my back now, I watch the sky
make wool pictures of mothers.

Two blackbirds fly toward the river:
the muddy river of endless regret.

I could lie here forever
and look up at these hollyhocks.

I will never get on in the world.

TWO BEERS IN
ARGYLE, WISCONSIN

Birds fly in the broken windows
of the hotel in Argyle.
Their wings are the cobwebs
of abandoned lead mines.

Across the street at Skelly's
the screen door bangs against the bricks
and the card games last all day.

Another beer truck comes to town,
chased by a dog on three legs.

Batman lies drunk in the weeds.

FRAGMENTS FROM AN
ILLINOIS SCRAPBOOK

1
Drum-taps of rain all night long.
2
In Nauvoo the grapes have been picked
and wine bottles wait in blue cellars.

3
Ghosts of bearded chicken farmers
are kneeling under the Mormon trees.
Their boots are crisscrossed with blood.
4
Clapboard houses in Knox County
contain girls who married Mozart.
5
Men who loved Stevenson and Altgeld
are singing hymns to Jesus
in coal towns south of Effingham.
6
The Rock River moon goes to bed
in the wigwam of a leaf.
7
Drum-taps of rain all night long.

THE FORGOTTEN GRAVEYARD

I have left my townsmen down below
under the shadows of Town Hall:
religious fakers, Republicans,
the windbags at the barbershop.

On this hill, the clean smell of skunk.

The ape-faced trees crouch like gnarled bootblacks
over the yellow tombstones;
and there is a bird's nest — a torn blue wig.

But I am at home among the dead,
the deformed, the discolored.

A woodpecker joyfully carves his hole.

The sunset sweetens the mouth of a leaf.

THE UNFOUND DOOR

. . . and all the sad and secret flowing of my life.

THOMAS WOLFE

Here in falling Kane County
the gold red brown leaves
drift down slowly slowly
like ships boats sinking

The air is blue bright blue

Oceans seas should be this blue

Oceans should have leaves
falling over them falling
in the rusty noons of fall

The gold red brown leaves
leave their old moorings
and drift off to a strange sea
where men are laughing in cornfields

I too am drifting and sinking
in the slow autumn weather
of Kane County Illinois

But I know now I know now
it is first love of this place
I want to hang on to

WEST OF CHILDHOOD

For My Brother, George Gardner

West of our childhood rote usurps the rites of spring,
    the wild sweet
season is an act of year. Uniformed robins
    hop and tweet
in chorus and culls from showgirls of seed catalogues doll
    up the view,
embellishing our Garden Homes, while Latin shrubs
    perform on cue.

A child's fierce focused gaze can wholly enter
and instantly become the bold gold center
of a single crocus, a listening child is fused to the
    sole voice
of that particular inimitable bird whose red
    choice
breast is robiner than never, a child perceives
the slow resolving of the one bud to the very leaf
of leaves.

East of now and years from Illinois the shout of spring
    out-rang the dinner bell.
Brother do you remember the walled garden, our dallies
    in that ding dong dell
where my fistful of violets mazed the air we moved
    through and upon
and a swallow of brook skimmed your tabloid sloop to
    sea and gone?
North of tomorrow your daughter's daughter's ears will
    ding with spring, wild
violets will forest in her fist scenting towns of space; and
    my son's child
(weddings from this suburb) will, with crocus eyes,
    flower other Mays:
That bud will leaf again, that choice bird sing, and paper
boats sail down the robin days.

CHILDREN ARE GAME

I have come often to this forest,
home to these never not green trees.
Now, in a grove of auburn bones

the spindling skeletons of summer flowers,
I hear the soft snow hiss through fir and spruce,
the shrill quick children skating on the pond
a safe and thousand miles from reef and shark.
What wings will whistle down this resined bark,
what monstrous blooming blast belief?
Children should not come to grief.
I swore that even crows could sing —
I thawed my winters thinking spring
and now am always cold, with reason,
for bombs can blossom any season.
The pheasant's chicks scratch posted ground,
children are game the whole year round
skating the thin ice of the pond
gay and innocent and spruce:
while I in a grave of once-were flowers
and stiffer than their thready bones
forget these seen to be green trees
too mindful of the forest.

OF FLESH AND BONE

Child and girl each morning summer winter or dismay
my eyes saw waterfalls my ears heard madrigals I ta-
sted strawberries touched moss smelt hay and roses, and
     through the blue
the bright sky I with my first and once-love flew.
Willow-boned sun-marrowed and air-skinned,
sea-water in my veins, I drank wine and the southwest
     wind.
The noun death and the verb to die were exiled from my

vocabulary, and when the salty boys and sun-burned
     girls I
mooned with on the honeysuckled porch through locust-
loud and sigh-soft summer nights did speculate upon the
     disposition of my dust
I said to them I am a girl of flesh and bone, my shift's
     no shroud,
and d-e-a-t-h is the word I do not say out loud.
That is the word I said that I will not admit.
(I had read of a fatal Irish ghost named IT
who reeked corruption and whose gaze was potent as
     the basilisk,
and IT became my parlor slang for the noun I dared
     not risk)
The salty boys bugled desire to die at thirty-five
and the girls harped a lust to be buried, not old maimed
     and alive.
I vowed that eyeless earless loinless lonely,
I would refuse to die; that even if only
one sense was left me, touch or smell or taste,
I would choose to live; that in a sewer of waste
a thicket of pain a mountain of fear or the sea-
wrack of sorrow I would beg, steal, and betray to be.
Girl and child my nightmare was the ceasing,
not the attendant pinch and panic, but the releasing
of the I. Now that my blood's a sweeter blend,
now that my bones are bones and do not bend,
now that my skin is dressed, what sucks my marrow
is not the final fact of IT but the engagement some
     tomorrow.

The certainty, in spite of locking doors and looking in
    the closets, that IT may wait
around That corner, under an unfamiliar bed, or through
    next summer's gate.
the meeting of ITS gaze in a sick second's shock of infi-
    nite danger
and then the slow or sudden but unrefusable embrace
    and the intolerable anger.
I am not faith-less but with those who see no future in
    eternity I do agree;
no paradise and no inferno will resolve the coming noth-
    ingness of me.
Mice and lions also die but God spared beasts our
    "knowing that we know"
today and yesterday, tomorrow, creeds and crimes ago.

Now mornings are still miracles and my dear now-love
    is my true
love and we fly we fly . . . O the sky was never once so
    bright and blue
and I still wish to live with living's theft-
ing and assault if even one sense will be left,
but to escape the meals and miles of waiting
I might elect the hour of my negating
and sleep peacefully to death some winter night,
cold finally to morning and to mourners and to fright.
Still, flesh and bone is wilful, and this knowledge is dead-
    certain and my horror,
that I shall not close my eyes when ITS eyes stare out of
    mine in every mirror.

THE MILKMAN

The door was bolted and the windows of my porch
were screened to keep invaders out, the mesh of rust-
proof wire sieved the elements. Did my throat parch
then sat I at my table there and ate with lust
most chaste, the raw red apples; juice, flesh, rind and
    core.

One still and summer noon while dining in the sun
I was poulticing my thirst with apples, slaking care,
when suddenly I felt a whir of dread. Soon, soon,
stiff as a bone, I listened for the Milkman's tread.
I heard him softly bang the door of the huge truck
and then his boots besieged my private yard. I tried
to keep my eyes speared to the table, but the suck
of apprehension milked my force. At last he mounted
my backstairs, climbed to the top, and there he stood still
outside the bolted door. The sun's color fainted.
I felt the horror of his quiet melt me, steal
into my sockets, and seduce me to him from
my dinner. His hand clung round the latch like rubber.
I felt him ooze against the screen and shake the frame.
I had to slide the bolt; and thus I was the robber
of my porch. Breathing smiling shape of fright,
the Milkman made his entrance; insistent donor,
he held in soft bleached hands the bottled sterile fruit,
and gave me this fatal, this apostate dinner.
Now in winter I have retreated from the porch
into the house and the once red apples rot where
I left them on the table. Now if my throat parch
for fruit the Milkman brings a quart for my despair.

THE WIDOW'S YARD

"Snails lead slow idyllic lives . . ."
The rose and the laurel leaves
in the raw young widow's yard
were littered with silver. Hard-
ly a leaf lacked the decimal scale
of the self of a snail. Frail
in friendship I observed with care
these creatures (meaning to spare
the widow's vulnerable eyes
the hurting pity in my gaze).

Snails, I said, are tender skinned.
Excess in nature . . . sun rain wind
are killers. To save themselves
snails shrink to shelter in their shells
where they wait safe and patient
until the elements are gent-
ler. And do they not have other foes?
the widow asked. Turtles crows
foxes rats, I replied, and canned
heat that picnickers aband-
on. Also parasites invade
their flesh and alien eggs are laid
inside their skins. Their mating
too is perilous. The meeting
turns their faces blue with bliss
and consummation of this
absolute embrace is so
extravagantly slow
in coming that love begun

at dawn may end in fatal sun.
The widow told me that her
husband knew snail's ways and his gar-
den had been Eden for them. He
said the timid snail could lift three
times his weight straight up and haul
a wagon toy loaded with a whole
two hundred times his body's burden.
Then as we left the garden
she said that at the first faint chill
the first premonition of fall
the snails go straight to earth . . . excrete
the lime with which they then secrete
the opening in their shells . . . and wait for spring.
It is those little doors which sing,
she said, when they are boiled.
She smiled at me when I recoiled.

LETTER FROM SLOUGH POND

Here where you left me alone
the soft wind sighs through my wishbone
the sun is lapping at my flesh
I couple with the ripples of the fresh
pond water I am rolled by the roiling sea.
Love, in our wide bed, do you lie lonely?
The spoon of longing stirs my marrow
and I thank God this bed is narrow.

PART OF THE DARKNESS

I had thought of the bear in his lair as fiercely free,
    feasting on honey and wildwood fruits;
I had imagined a forest lunge, regretting the circus
    shuffle and the zoo's proscribed pursuits.
Last summer I took books and children to Wisconsin's
    Great North woods. We drove
one night through miles of pines and rainy darkness to
    a garbage grove
that burgeoned broken crates and bulging paper bags
    and emptied cans of beer,
to watch for native bears, who local guides had told us,
    scavenged there.
After parking behind three other cars (leaving our head-
    lights on but dim)
We stumbled over soggy moss to join the families blink-
    ing on the rim
of mounded refuse bounded east north and west by the
    forest.
The parents hushed and warned their pushing children
    each of whom struggled to stand nearest
the arena, and presently part of the darkness humped
    away from the foliage and lumbered bear-shaped
toward the heaping spoilage. It trundled into the litter
    while we gaped,
and for an instant it gaped too, bear-faced, but not a
    tooth was bared. It grovelled
carefully while tin cans clattered and tense tourists tit-
    tered. Painstakingly it nosed and ravelled
rinds and husks and parings, the used and the refused;
    bear-skinned and doggedly explored

the second-hand remains while headlights glared and
    flashlights stared and shamed bored
children booed, wishing aloud that it would trudge away
    so they might read its tracks.
They hoped to find an as yet unclassified spoor, certain
    that no authentic bear would turn his back
upon the delicacies of his own domain to flounder where
    mere housewives' leavings rot.
I also was reluctant to concede that there is no wild
    honey in the forest and no forest in the bear.
Bereaved, we started home, leaving that animal there.

THIS ROOM IS FULL OF CLOCKS

I am trying to write at a desk that is mine
these mornings thanks to the kindness of a stranger.
His room is full of clocks. All of them are ticking.
I fumble through a folder of abandoned poems
and of news stories I cut from papers I must
have conned some enterprising morning years ago.

Here is the account of a rare black swan that flew
from somewhere to Waukegan Harbor to a Greek
café where "it huddled at the door its feathers
drenched with oil." The swan was sad reports the paper,
    so Mathon
Kyritsis, restaurant keeper and fisherman,
consulted an ornithologist who said the
sorry bird was one of one hundred nineteen Black
Australian Swans that still survive and that the bird
could not live in captivity without its mate.

No doubt this Rare Swan died of fatigue let alone
bereavement even before I snipped the clippings.
Perhaps Mr. Kyritsis lives telling his tale . . .
The paper did not give the age of Mathon K.

Here's a clipping with the heading ANIMALS:
HOW OLD THEY GET. It is an accounting from "the
reliable records of zoos, aquariums
and aviaries all over the world," offered
with comments by the Cook County Forest Preserve.
For instance it says here that "man is longer lived
than any other mammal," and sure enough the
record shows a pampered elephant only made
it to sixty-nine. It is different for some
of our poets. MacNeice and Roethke have died
at fifty-five just like the Giant Salamander
while an occasional catfish is alive at
sixty. I don't begrudge the turkey-buzzard his
one hundred and eighteen years, nor the swan who if
he has his mate can live to one hundred and two
(that rare Black Swan who flew to Waukegan did not)
but I mind reading that coddled alligators
(safe from such random killers as love or neglect)
are able to thrash and lash and grin at sixty-eight.
Even in these days no Thomas, Cummings, Roethke
or MacNeice have managed that. It is possible
that there should be a Forest Preserve for poets
each with his or her mate but I remind myself
that the poet is rumoured to be less constant
than the swan. No the bard must do his best with book
and bed and booze and blunders of the heart and
bearing witness burying friends banning bombs
and using onomatopeia with restraint.

JAMES HEARST *was reared on a farm in Black Hawk County, Iowa, three miles west of Cedar Falls. He has been publishing poems for more than thirty years, and has gathered them in four books:* Country Men *(1937, and 1943 with some new poems),* The Sun at Noon *(1943),* Man and His Field *(1951), and* Limited View *(1962, 1963). He was educated at the State College of Iowa, University of Iowa and, in Mexico, at the University of Guanajuato. In addition to supervising his large farm, he teaches creative writing and literature at the State College of Iowa.*

LIMITED VIEW

The clutter and ruck of the stubble publish the time
That prompts my steps, I know what I have to do
For my bread before frost locks the land against
My hand, and fire shoulders the chimney flue.

Rocks have a word that crows repeat over and over
On the cold slopes of winter where the picking is poor.
It echoes in empty granaries and I learn by heart
To say in the hard days to come, endure, endure.

But now I straddle the field and break its back
In the vise of my plow, while a thresh of weather
    streams by
Sweeping up clouds and birds, leaves, banners of smoke;
I gouge out furrows, a starved wind ransacks the sky.

FARM HAND

A mule with fork and shovel breeds no honey
for spring triggered girls to buzz around
though he wear overalls and hate his muscles.

Sweat marks name me, not the moth
that longs for perfume in white bells
and dusts love pollen after dark.

The cracked and aching heart
of my desire, plain on my face
as a smear of fresh dug earth,

bleeds foolishly while sleight of hand
salesmen with instructed mirrors
make me pay for what I see.

So sober I, tied to my stake,
chew the grass within my circle
and shake my long ears at the moon.

LANDMARK

The road wound back among the hills of mind
Rutted and worn, in a wagon with my father
Who wore a horsehide coat and knew the way
Toward home, I saw him and the tree together.

For me now fields are whirling in a wheel
And the spokes are many paths in all directions,
Each day I come to crossroads after dark,
No place to stay, no aunts, no close connections.

Calendars shed their leaves, mark down a time
When chrome danced brightly. The roadside tree is rotten,
I told a circling hawk, widen the gate
For the new machine, a landmark's soon forgotten.

You say the word, he mocked, I'm used to exile.
But the furrow's tongue never tells the harvest true,
When my engine saw had redesigned the landscape
For a tractor's path, the stump bled what I knew.

THE TARNISH

The afternoon failed of its promise and the sun
Hid in a thicket of clouds on its downward climb,
The bright day's petals tattered and fell apart
Lost as a tower clock's voice asleep at its chime.

I rocked on my heels and saw sleet's rowdy hands
Rumple the tulip bed, a cold wind goaded
A child at play till she cried, I turned to stare
At a shallow hill where the topsoil had eroded.

The small mean faults of the day like blisters broken
Rubbed raw, were slow to heal, I felt time's wedge
Split need from the order of things, like a farm run down
By shabby intentions, a plow with a rusty edge.

My pride reads omens in mischief and my hand tosses
Entrails of stunted dreams in the air as portents,
I carry my doctor's degree on such occasions
And speak at length on the tarnish of small losses.

TRUTH

How the devil do I know
if there are rocks in your field,
plow it and find out.
If the plow strikes something
harder than earth, the point
shatters at a sudden blow
and the tractor jerks sidewise
and dumps you off the seat —
because the spring hitch
isn't set to trip quickly enough
and it never is — probably
you hit a rock. That means
the glacier emptied his pocket
in your field as well as mine,
but the connection with a thing
is the only truth that I know of,
so plow it.

CHANGE TOWARD CERTAINTY

The afternoon closed in until it seemed
No larger than a room of snow and cloud,
The small March sun glowed dimly in its socket,
The window of the air looked out on mist.
I met you there among the apple trees
Close to the feedlot where the playful steers
Rumpled the bedding in their narrow pen,
And starlings searched the ground for spilled out grain

Like careful business men, the fog was a wall.
Oh, we were all prisoners of the day
Though some found fences more substantial than
The feeling. I was centered in my mood,
Your warm appraising look slid off my back.
Like quicksand underneath our boots the snow
Shifted as we sank deeper in our coats.
Look, and you pointed to a maple tree
Where swollen buds now showed a waxy red,
I looked from where bare ground defied the frayed
Snow carpet, then you said, There's not much yet.
I felt the wind, not freezing, raw and wet.
A ghostly crow in the fog spoke his short piece
With nothing new to say, I looked at you
And saw your hair curl lively from your scarf
Framing your face where the excitement grew
Out of an anxious frown as if a light
Had come to light blind eyes, your mittened hand
Turned snug in mine like a child's while a shadow went
Away from your face, and the actual bodies of things
Filled up the space where their shadows had seemed
        to be.
Nothing seemed changed and yet the change was there
In the tree, in the bird, in you and I felt your love
Beat in me like a pulse I had always known.

THE GREAT COINCIDENCE

How strange that in the human flow,
And think of the people we have met,
That out of the many ways to go,
And think of those untraveled yet,

We should, enclosed in time and place
Like two in a dream, come face to face.

I marvel every day that we
With our own hearts escaped the fate
Of those who pass and do not see.
We stopped before it was too late
And tired the distance we could reach
Across the unknown each to each.

It is a wonder that we came
So close that we could learn together
The odds and pleasures of the game
We daily play with time and weather,
That we two joined in one defense
I call the great coincidence.

BURN THE COCOONS

The sun waits in the sky for me
as I crawl slowly toward his feet
dragging the field I'm working in
that will be finished when we meet.

All day across the field I've come,
the seeder's whine my only note,
shivering as an east wind picks
the berry of flesh inside my coat.

The rising tide of sap has furred
the maple twigs with fires of green
burning away the grey cocoons
webbed on my eyes till I have seen

the land that I have got to sow
stretch like a plain into the sun
filled with crops I hope to grow
out of the seeding I've begun.

SNAKE IN THE STRAWBERRIES

This lovely girl dressed in lambswool thoughts
dances a tune in the sunshine, a tune like a bright path
leading to the soft cloud curled up like a girl
in her sleep, but she stops at the strawberry bed
carrying nothing but joy in her basket and it falls
to the ground. O-h—h—h—h, her red lips round out
berries of sound but the berries under her feet are
not startled though they sway ever so slightly
as life long striped and winding congeals into
form, driving its red tongue into her breast
forever marking its presence and turning into a shiver
barely a thread of motion in the clusters of green leaves.
She stands now as cold as marble now with the thought
coiled around her, the image of her thought holding her
tightly in its folds for it is part of her now and dimly
like faint sobbing she knows that part of her crawls
forever among green leaves and light grasses, it is the
        same
shiver that shakes her now and now her hair
        tumbles slightly
and now she feels dishevelled but the spell breaks finally.
For the warm sun has not changed and maybe the tune
of her coming still floats in the air but the path
no longer ends in the cloud. She fills her basket taking

the richest ripe berries for this is what she came to do
she touches her breast a minute and then the ground
feeling beneath her fingers the coiled muscles
of a cold fear that seems so dark and secret
beside the warm colors of the sunlight
splashing like blood on the heaped fruit in her basket.

CLOVER SWATHS

My eyes are cloudy with death.

I saw thirty acres of clover fall over the sickle bar
today (not the Grim Reaper, but a bright steel sickle
out of IHC, guaranteed for sixty days against
faulty or defective workmanship.)

Thirty acres of clover in full bloom died today,
beside such incidentals as a hen pheasant with
both legs cut off, her eggs decorating horses' hooves,
and only God can count the number of bob-o-links
and meadowlarks that find their world levelled.

Thirty acres of clover just in its prime,
in its greatest flower, this field —
lusty, sweet smelling, the seed nodes filling . . .

Tonight when I go for the cows
I shall see it lying there in flat definite swaths.

(Only the young men go to war.)

ROBERT HUFF *was born in Evanston, Illinois, and was educated at Wayne State and Indiana universities. He holds an M.A. from Wayne State and has taught there. He presently teaches at Western Washington State College. His work appears frequently in such magazines as* Paris Review, Saturday Review, Altantic Monthly, Northwest Review, Harper's, Poetry Magazine, Prairie Schooner *and* Voices, *and he has published two volumes:* Colonel Johnson's Ride and Other Poems *(1959) and* The Course *(1966). Poems of his have been printed in a Bore-stone Mountain Poetry Award book (1957) and in a number of anthologies.*

EARLY SNOW

I

The early snow had come at night, perched
In the trees and fluttered to the ground.
At first it fell like feathers and the farm
Took on the silence easily, no sound
Of wings but whiteness in the air
Around the silo, frosty trees. And then
A breeze, the flurries, and the wind beating
The feathers till they flew the farmyard
Like great flocks of birds, frightened and landing
White on everything. By morning, sunlight
Woke her, but she knew the snow had fallen.
It was too still, much too heavy in her ears.

She looked at him and waited. But their room
Was cold with waiting, like the tomb before
The stone gave way, before the dawnlight paced
Death's linen sleep and shook the dark blood

Of eternity. And when he turned
She had avoided him, moved to the cold
Edge of the bed where she could listen
For the waking sounds of morning
As it touched the animals. Then light was
On the rooster with its golden pillars
Diving in the hay, the old light still
Diagonal, on the rise, bold in the fields

Of first snow once again. She would have asked him,
But it was no use. Why ask her husband
How it felt to know the geese would soon be
Scuttled stars, the earth and sky one color
Till they moved and found their footprints followed them?
Down to the roots life went, plunged out of sight
All winter, out of bounds. The gander flocked
His white cheeks with a tail wind south over
The lunging trees. Soon nothing but the hawk,
Her husband's bird, winging his grey shark's belly
Like the ghost of some mad fisher in the sky,
Would fly his airtight circles heavenward.

And Roger would be happy in the white-willed
Winter weather of the hawk. The three
Would be alone, so he could talk of Noah
And the Ark that rode out God's wrath when the world
Was water and that holy sea bubbled
The blue Almighty through man's lungs. Already
It was lonely on the cold edge of the bed.
The room was bright with morning, and she listened
To him breathing quietly. She eased away,
Dressed quickly, found his gun, and left the house

Before he was awake. Walking across
The new snow she could hear the gander squawk.

The geese had always walked like drinking men,
Not drunkards, but determined, waddling
As if they knew they had to get some place.
And she remembered Roger when he drank,
Braced up and tried to speak of love to her:
"Does my sweet country lady wing marsh hens?
Whatever was in the beginning sends
The noisy bittern lopping through the fog,
Born half sweet Jesus . . . one half crawling log . . . .
Phyllis, my bare feet nailed me for a frog.
Mosquitoes know it; pestilence still sings
For blood and honey, Phyl . . . but wings! Their sting

"Hold early childhood festered . . . . One red boil
Throbs under all my birthdays, strains and spoils
My shirts, Phyl, stains the shirt I wear . . .
Unless the pond returns . . . comes like the sea . . . .
How fond are feathers, Phyl? In Galilee
They quieted the sea, but Christ tossed
Nicodemus water wings . . . . Lost in the sea . . .
Unless I say, 'I love you, Phyllis.' . . . Oh,
Sweet Phyl, come home with me. Thou art
Beloved now." She took him home that night,
Helped him undress, and got him into bed.
So she recalled his drunken tenderness.

His body, heavy in the darkness, begged
Her body closer, and she came to him,
The blessed, floating nest, ark of the flesh
And spirit bearing dawn. Month after month

It happened as their mornings came and went.
Harvest by seed and sun time, Roger took
The strength she lent him and was gone
Into the fields to work or hunt. It left
Her weak and empty, far away by evening
As he told her little stories of the hawk,
Alone before the frowning, boyish face
That manned the Bible when the sun went down.

II

The snow itself had crept into the barn.
It sifted through loose shingles, falling
Softly in the hayloft. On the clover,
Down along the ladder rungs, it lay
Like powder, glistened in the light that leaked
Between the weathered walls. Roger stopped short
And listened, but the sounds were cattle feeding,
Chicken noise, the wind rattling the door.
"All done," he said aloud, "all settled down."
And to himself: "It is all settled here."
The Jersey mooed. "All certain," Roger thought,
Taking the warm milk with him from the barn.

He thought about his wife. There were her tracks,
Fresh, straight across the field, diminishing
Before him as he stared into the snowlight.
Then a shadow moved across them, and he
Knew the bird was waiting for a gift
Of ripe intestines, rabbit heads. The sky
Was always stalking hungry life, hawking
The fled, the hunter. And the animals
Twitched backward in their fall. The shadow gambled

With his memory, wheeled past the red beak
Feeding, footprints, snow; turning him like
An old wheel with a crooked, bouncing ball

It left him spinning at the farmhouse door.
He drank his coffee whiskied. It was so.
Life was a hunting, hunted, running thing,
Betting on love and godless realized.
It was. She left him with a stoic bird,
Ran for the wild fowl like a moon-struck girl.
There was some half-dammed creature in those eyes
That watched him as he read to her,
Waited for spring and trammeled Eastertide.
It was no way in winter, but she'd gone
Back for a last look, gone outside,
As if those geese were set on paradise.

He took the bottle to the living room,
Sat by the window waiting her return
Across the north field. Who had failed
The seasons? Which gone wrong? The trail was there,
The shadow. It was so. It was absurd
To marry, drift away, and clutch at nothing
Sound as memory. But through the window
Sunlight on the snow blazed the white hay field,
Blinding, and he thought he saw her walking
Through the field summers ago. The strange north light
Came closer, brought her near. An evening glow.
It felt like summer as he went to her.

Before they fell asleep the change began.
The dark wind twisting through the maze of hay
Stopped, sudden as a whisper, and was gone
Behind the clover when the north horizon

Shivered like a dyke, gave up the tide,
And dawn shot through the night sky over them.
They saw the Cub go under; then Charles' Wain,
Caught in the glare that widened as it rose,
Tossed with the starry bones of the Great Bear,
Sank slowly in the white flood and was lost.
"God's fall," he thought, "the craft of heaven here,
The cost of marriage, drowning, after all."

It crossed the sky dead center, darkness south
Clutching the southern trees, until the trees
Were swamped-clean silhouettes of ships aground
Slapped by the northern sea, with black masts pointing
Through the breaker's light and all their canvas
Flapping, frozen green. "Roger," she said, "don't speak
Now, not a word; don't look down," and he heard
Her move to him, the Northern Lights' dawn-ghost,
Ichthyosaur, enticing fish, immortal
In the sky. She whispered: "I am your wife, Rog,
Your love . . . ." Then black above them once again.
The abstract constellations racked the stars

For keepsakes of Aurora racing through
The arctic night, the dim stars; and the wind
Back in the hay where they lay quiet, drowned
Now, or asleep, lay landlocked with the dew
Standing in beads along the clover. Light
Was still in darkness on the flock of hens
That looked like whitewashed stones, cold on the bones
Beside the dog, and on the crooked pitchfork
Hardly moved. The barnyard held that summer night
As though the north horizon could not spawn

The least light on the earth until the rooster
Told the dawn the farm was rolling east.

But they had seen the sky change and the white,
Shaft ceiling rising to the arch carry
The plow away before their eyes: The winged
Word then a polar ecstasy with upward
Fathoms cradled in the clear dome of the sky —
Round, absolute, consumed humanity —
Not like the sky the geese flew when the haze
Was full of bloodhounds, and she chased
The baying vision that arose
And was still movement at the close,
Migration of praised feathers in a packed
V that was maddening grey on grey.

III
The borrowed shotgun fascinated her.
Polished and blue it was with one gold bead
Which nestled on the barrel, a tiny yellow
Pointer like a false egg, dead, rubbed bright,
With lead balls full of darkness crouched inside.
She squinted down the barrel at the sky,
Swinging the gun from cloud to cloud and down
At treetops where the shapeless blue crumbled
And formed its artificial leaves. The sky
Was empty, silent, bare before the gun
She held as if it were a gold-tipped wand.
Then there was something rising in the trees.

A shadow, winged, nearly translucent span,
Rose in the blue and spiralled up. The hawk
Alone had seen her from his high place
In the cedars and was moving into space

To watch her cross the meadow toward the wheat
The flock of geese was feeding on. And they
Were hidden there, over the knoll, expecting
Nothing but the straight north wind, ready
To move ahead of it before the late snow
Came and left the fields a white waste, haunted,
Bleak, scanned by the patient falcon whose one plan
Was that his beak taste the invisible.

Roger had left the house, followed her tracks
Along the fence, and started through the hay field
After her. This was the very spot where they
Had been. Packed under three years' marriage
In the frozen loam and thick glaze of the snow,
The haystack they had ridden raged again
Below his heavy boots; electric, fast
Beneath him, he could feel the tide rip back
The maze to set him bobbing in that summer's foam.
His legs churned snow. She had to realize
That he had found out, got her back; forgive
Him for lost weather and the burned-out nights

That frightened him with fish turned flyers
In a flaming sea. The geese were restless
When she reached the knoll; scouting the air
With bills of rooted wheat, they turned uneasy
Necks, sprouts serpenting. Phyllis could hear
The lead bird call. She crawled up, noiseless,
Slow, peered down. And there he was, the great male
With his throng, their long necks wrapped in his will,
And she saw him flapping, ready to be gone.
It had happened suddenly. She flew at him,
Brandished the gold bead, cocked, pointed, and froze
Still as a snowman in the squawking whir

That rushed and slapped the air, stirring the sky
Black: shafts, then arrowhead. She melted
With the gun leaned on her breast, softly, alone,
The silence hovering. Something aloft
Then, where the geese had been, came over her,
Almost a swimming bird. Roger could see
Them now, girl waiting, hawk. He walked on faster.
It was a mistake. The bird must have mistaken
Her for him. She had no scraps to offer,
Yet the wings swept down close to her, and he saw
Her raise the gun and fire twice. The hawk
Bounced, drooped, in slipstream met the earth.

Roger was shouting, but she couldn't hear;
Her ears heard nothing when she reached the bird
But strange sounds, distant, dreadful. One crazed eye
Was staring at her, still alive and staring
At the sky, she thought at first, but no, at her.
It glared up like a bright ball, branded, burned
Her deep and deeper, and she raised the gun butt
In the air, lashed out, and struck the throbbing bird
Blow after blow until the head was smashed.
He found her kneeling, tried to speak to her,
Knelt down beside her, dumb, sobbing, dumb,
Watching her kiss the dead wings in the snow.

JOHN KNOEPFLE *was born in Cincinnati, Ohio,
studied at Dartmouth College and received his Ph. B.
from Xavier University in 1947 and his M.A. in English
in 1949. For two years he was producer-director at an
educational TV station in Cincinnati. He has taught at
Ohio State University, Southern Illinois University,*

Washington University and Maryville College, among other schools, and presently teaches at St. Louis University. His poetry has been published in Colorado Quarterly, Chicago Review, Commonweal, The Nation, America, Yale Review, *and many other publications, and his first volume* Rivers Into Islands *was published in 1965.*

ST. LOUIS MIDDAY

Sucking at summer
the black face
floats in the noon
heat. It moves
through hard dust and labor,
not conscious
of its own shadow.
It does not even know
the yellow lizards
crippled in its eyes.

He stacks bricks
in the hot day.
The headache ball
breaks down his home.

HAMPTON ROAD

Lean sabre jets
hatch in the fenders
of forgotten chevrolets
where teenagers

burning with the sun
crash through drive-in windows.
The radio
dredges an old channel
among obsolete songs.

LATE SHIFT IN THE MILL

The mill seethes
when the shift breaks.
Eyes of rats in smokeholes
burn ruby when the workers
throw crumbs to the walls.

The men pitch slag
that wounds the streaking
balls and claws.
They leave the cripples
dragging for the ravenous.

Arms bronzed, faces
stained in caves of fire,
they swing through miles of steel
the cold
carbuncular night.

OLD MOON PLANTER

We needed the moon.
Whipped our mules all day
while the sun whipped us,
and left those fields spilled

over sod with black
soil. And full mooned nights
we drove our wives there
yelling hi-ki-wee
ki-wee-ah and they
running like stark does
down the naked land.
And when they winded
we buckled their knees
and took them on top
those furrows milky
with their great moons full.
Then the green corn came
like mad I'll tell you.

CHURCH OF ROSE OF LIMA, CINCINNATI

It looks from the hill like something
Fra Angelico painted, the red
rectangular lines and the bricked bell
steepled out of time. This church
honors Saint Rose in a city
as spare of Peruvians as miracles.

It floods out whenever the river rises
and has a smell of common water
at the altars, and pilots of tows
on long hauls from Pennsylvania
needle the dark with searching lights
to catch the hour off her clock.

Saint Rose keeps a timid time.
I've heard her bell strike three
as if an afternoon surprised her.
The church itself may well surprise her.
In Lima she has golden altars; Germans
made them wood on the unliturgical river.

But churches anywhere seem rude for her.
This virgin kept a hidden time
and the world could give no wedding ring
to wed her with. Her lover came quick
and killed the Peruvian roses she grew fond of
and the small buds withered in the winter fog.

Once I thought the rococo Christ
had made her a violent dove and held
her trembling in his hand like a bell.
I am not so sure of this today.
She may be undiscoverable, like silt
slow rivers encourage into islands.

NIGHT FIRE

Above the oil refinery
the torch howls in the wind,
flaring and contracting
among the millionaires.
It snaps there.

Smoke trails underneath it,
and I think it resembles
a severed head on a platter,
a John Baptist lurid in sparkles
of Bedouin handbells.
I drive down the road,
then it leaps up again,
grinning in the car mirror
like a colored porter in a plush hotel,
or a flame that roars in its solitude.

EDWARDSVILLE
BEFORE SUNRISE

"Portals-of-prayer"
turns my clock radio on
and I am consoled
with the death of sparrows.
The bedroom windows are frozen
with obliterated stars.
A spider
embalmed in his ragged web
since the last September
is the king of that north.
My wife sleeps
a continent away.
Under the covers
my skin defines the strange
form of a man.

NORTH ON ONE-ELEVEN

The swamp alongside the road
fed a world so dark
I could not see it
when I drove there each night
due north for home.
Sometimes a thin moon in the east
dropped shafts of light
on the steel rails that crossed the road.
I learned to watch for this light
gliding for the crossing
at precisely the speed of the car.
I would argue with myself,
the moonlight is without substance,
then feel it slam my stomach
and splinter in my nerves
when I hit the rails.

Later I remembered that light,
thinking of Augustine,
raw meat on the hooks of time
when Vandals were breaking the gates
at Hippo, and I told myself
it is the Vandals who are dead,
but the mouth of the old saint
gleams with foxfire.

Now tonight
the swamp fevers my road
and the moon is put out
and my headlights pierce the dark

with beams riven into the banks of fog,
and I raise my arm
warding a blow.

HEMAN AVENUE HOLIDAY

When these georgian apartments are leveled,
bits of plaster clinging to the rooms we knew,
we will crawl naked from the stones of our cellars.
We will crawl up into the light, and among us
there will be pensioners and cooks and musicians,
and we will join together, as in a congregation.
We will not have any names and no identities.
We will have only our sadness for a little while,
the nipples yearning, secret whorls of the hair exposed,
the genitals designed with no further purpose,
the navels mysterious, meaningless, and we will go
and lie down in two long rows on the burnt grass
where the mall was with its cool green sycamores.
We will gather scraps of paper to rest ourselves on,
tissues, the halves of torn letters, school notes,
the waste of our generation on that long mall,
and we will pretend that if someone came with bread
we would not destroy each other for the broken crumbs.
No, we will die together in a greatness of our souls.

JUNE NIGHT ON THE RIVER

Tonight the river is
calm enough. A string of cars
drums the long Eads Bridge
toward Union Station.

Pullman windows
charge the secret
spans of the bridge and tall
lights travel over the water.
They are hooded monks
gleaming among the piers.

Now I see whole mountains
honeycombed with monks,
and one of these, a boy
from Athos, fills the blue
Aegean with his own
image as he leans
beyond the prow of his skiff
and tries his luck
with a hooked line for his life,
his serious gesture.

The train goes its way,
the long lights
go out. I pour myself
a careful beer, tilting
a cold glass above
the Mississippi. It is
a lost river roiling
underneath the bridge. It came
from a deep cave on this
June night. And still it is
the one river Clemens
gave his own true Huck,
head buried in the black
knees of Jim, and the same
winds howl down streaks
of our summer storms.

JOSEPH LANGLAND *was born in Spring Grove, Minnesota, and educated at Santa Ana College and the University of Iowa. He teaches at the University of Massachusetts, and has been a guest professor at various universities. He has published three volumes —* The Green Town (Poets of Today III), *which was a nominee for the National Book Award,* The Wheel of Summer, *which won the Melville Cane Award, and* Adlai Stevenson. *Also he co-edited the anthologies* The Short Story *and* Poet's Choice. *His work has appeared in some of the anthologies and in many magazines, including* Atlantic Monthly, The New Yorker, London Magazine, *the* Nation *and in the* Hudson, Paris, *and* Massachusetts *reviews.*

THE WHEEL OF SUMMER

The dark land rose in the luminous arch of sky.
The bald sun softly grew. Down by the barn
My father and we three sons watched how it fell
Through hazes of sour dust by the old pig pens.
"They got away from us," my father said.
He didn't need to say it. The great sun god
Bowed to the grassy sea by the western hills,
Darkened to blood, rolled in the tasseled corn
And flamed our blinking eyeballs. "Yup," we said,
And turned in the dirty twilight to our thoughts.

    Those silken shoats with jiggling nuts
    Went squealing under their mother's tits
    Two months too long, until they ran
    Smelling each other around the pens
    And snuffled into a herd of lusts.

Ourselves but fifteen, fourteen, twelve,
We knew that wrestling those young boars
And bearing them, sterile, up from the knives
With bristling feet and foaming mouths
Could bend our steel and twist our smiles.

We ambled, loose in overalls, up by the house.
We doused our barny hands in sun-warmed waters,
Waited for supper, glanced at the girls, then ate.
We counted a few odd stars and the evening star
Over the glut of summer. Later, upstairs,
We stripped and gathered a pillow into our arms,
Rolled in the humid nightfall once or twice,
Muttered a thing or two, then fell asleep.

The women swept the kitchen,
Carried the washing waters,
Scrubbing towels and basins.
We slept. They quietly chatted,
Loosened their hair and spread it
In puffs for summer dreaming.

Out of those dreaming coves
The dawn broke, suddenly,
And rolled the milk-dust haze
Up Bekkan's Ridge. We yawned,
Straightened the slack in our mouths,
Tightened our muscles a notch,
Wrinkled our groins like a gourd,
And marched on out to the barn.

Then father called, "Let's drive them in."
We harried pigs toward the dusty barn,
Kicked the shoats and rammed the door
And banged the bar in its wooden home.

Coarse as our job, we whaled them all
Till some walked, upright, on the gates
And flowed together. "Wet them down!"
In the stock-tank our buckets swam,
Slipped and swished and, bellying up,
Went shivering over the slithering pens.
Our badgered strength was out of mind
In summer madness: a sty of sounds.

Our father, priest and teacher, led us on.
We stood in the sire's circle while he talked,
Whipped out his knife and whetted it on stone.
He flipped some acrid lysol from his jug
To test it out, then touched the slicing blade
Gingerly over his thumb. All set to go.
"Boys, let's bring them on." We'd bring them on.

We eyed the mob,
Curious, queasy.
Grey dust flowered
Under the rafters.
Breathy and muddy.
They surged together
In sour odors.

The three of us drove down the herd.
I grabbed one, dared not let him go.
Some boyish pride threw out my arms
To catch the unsuspecting world.
They clamped like iron. Crushing him,
I locked him to my chest and bore
Him, staggering, to the trough. Hair,
Plastered with dust, bristled my arms.

"Hup, flip him now!" Damned if I didn't,
But square on his feet. Off he ran,

His bony tail stretched outward from my hands,
He charged the herd. I hauled him down again,
And up from the pigsty floor we two arose,
Loudly embracing. And for what purposes?
"Hang on this time!" You think I would've lost him?
I knew when we were working, not at games,
When to be gentle, when to play it rough;
One cannot breed ten thousand animals
Into this world and woo them for the axe
Without a curse and prayer to help him through.

I got him upside down in the trough
And hung on his heels. I stomped his chest.
My brother locked his squealing snout.
With lysol, tender flesh was doused;
That knife dipped in the slickest stroke
I ever saw this side of hell,
And murderous music, like a crime,
Gurgled that milk-blue blooded dream.

Snip went the cords; the mindless body doubled.
Flick went the blade again; the shades of change
Rolled down the dust beyond the feeding troughs,
A tough abstraction. Dropping the crippled pig,
We rolled him out and ran him down the alley.
He walked so gingerly he seemed to dance
With quivering hooves upon the ragged straw
Along the barn. The solemn way he went,
He must have dumbly felt some ancient law
Driving him out of nature's benediction.

Infected with truth,
We hung in dust
Drenched to our skins,
Bleached to our bones.
He sat in the straw
Mute as a rock,
Crudely undone.
Ranker than swine,
Coarse to our nails
We swung to our job.

Then we went all the way
To common terms with loss.

Having run down our guilt and pain,
We lobbed the curses from our mouths.

We trapped them all. We never bore so much
Next to our hearts. We caught them with our feet,
Caged them for death and shrilled them back to life
To trot, untroubled, fattening for your grace.
So we prepared your table. The awful world
Seemed natural as breathing. Brazen with swine,
We hounded the living daylights out of the earth.
Nature we rolled, denatured, in the straw
Where loss waits in the alleys like a snake,
Coiled and ready, although it cannot strike.
The last lay down exhausted, wouldn't run.
We could have lain down with him. Had he fought
We might have, in our weakness, let him go.
At last, we spun the gates and turned them out
Under the burroak trees by the young alfalfa.

The barrows wandered through the blooming grasses.
We poured some water for their healing mudbaths.
We filled their troughs with generous sour mashes.
Burying snouts, they snuffled in rows of pigs' eyes,
And we, stinking high heaven, turned and trotted
Slowly along the woodpaths into the valley.

How shall I praise the valley waters,
The crystal springs so sweetly aching
Over our bruised, our lusty bodies?

We slid in water like sluggish wishes
And lay on sandbanks, mute and weary.
The water idled over our heartbeats.

We blew cool water out of our noses
With the clotted curses and gray mucus
And rose in our summer limbs for drying.

From sparkling stones we walked; then, dressing
In cleanest clothes on the polished gravels,
We stretched ourselves on yielding grasses,

While healing evening came.
We felt another dream
Rise in our flesh and feed
The mouth of mysteries;
It flickered in our minds
And quivered in our thighs.
Sweeping across our limbs,
It loosed our fumbling tongues
Until, at last, we talked
About the neighbor girls
And joked among ourselves.

We rose from the banks. For the evening star
Our casual wishes and shadowy groves
Welled with a tougher grace. To the barn
We rocked with the great maternal cows
And milked them down with our gentlest hands.

Next morning took us like an old surprise.
Fallen, with old corruption in our arms,
We praised the animal urgencies of love,
Our long obedience. The mind of man,
Boyishly wandering out of the eye of God,
Seemed natural to our wills. Our bruised bones
Took on this sweet admission. Proud in the sun,
Calloused and cocked, wicked and wise and young,
We ran, three golden idols, back to chores,
Shouldered the wheel of summer, and journeyed on.

SACRIFICE OF THE SPARROWS
OF THE FIELD

My mother and sisters washed out each other's
Hair in sweet lemons and purest rainwaters;
And so did the neighboring girls and their mothers,
Lounging on porchswings on long summer mornings.
    Whenever the rain fell
    They ran with pails full
    Of water from eavespouts
    Pouring in cisterns.
When I dribbled a milkwhitened pebble downward
Into the softwater well depth, it whispered
In circles of girlfaces, wreathed and laughing;
Maybe it didn't, and maybe it mattered.

But sparrows clogging
The eavetroughs hanging
Under our houses
Were clouding our waters.
Horse hair and barn straw and cow dung together
They wove into cozy egg homes as they twittered,
And downy cock feathers in scissor-beaks shredded,
With mosses and mudroots packed in for filler.
Dark summer showers
And spouting baubles
Broke from our shingles
On sisters and mothers.
Whenever straight hair hung stringy and oily
My father and brothers were cursing the sparrows,
And up in the rain went the twin-sliding ladders,
And down came the baby sparrows, splashing.
Naked wet sorrows,
Babes in my palms, then,
Bled out of tenderness.
Dying becalmed them.
God knew that they clogged the troughs with odd odors
And, filthy with lice from their barnridden feathers,
Strained to our wells. Then sisters' and mothers'
Hair hung unwashed on their breasts and their shoulders.
For whatever is hanging —
Angel or evil —
Over our eyelids,
God must be answering.
In a crown of sweet Sundays, their services psalming
In wreaths of hair-presses and redolent showers,
Golden and brown under summerlace bonnets,
The rainwater mothers and sisters are singing

Bird-warbled summer
And rain-washed dripping
In cisterns drumming.
Bless the sweet sinner,
But our fine rural ladies must wash in rainwater.
We climb in our world, all brothers and fathers,
And run where it bells us, attacking and loving,
To sing the pure Sunday of sisters and mothers.

And sleep out the years in the arms of our lovers.

CRANE

One day when childhood tumbled the spongy tufts
Banking the naked edge of our bottomlands
A shadowy sand-hill crane
Arose from Rocky Spring with a flipping fish,
A speckled rainbow,
Speared in her slim black bill.
She offered her wings in sluggish waves,
Wading impossibly up the slapping waters,
And ascended the crystal floods.

Under that dark ark
Two grappling anchors of dangling legs
Rolled away so smoothly the eye forgot them
Until that tall ungainly crane
Lay in the sky like a dream.
Her snaking head
Pivoted vaguely over our deep, green valley
And straightened to kiss the horizon.

Fish and crane
Swam through the white bowl of blue air,
Spinning outward upon
Mountainous heights and their soft mysterious pulleys.

My naked shoulders ached for the tumbling clouds,
And my shivering legs
Thrashed through those mossy fishing meadows,
Over the rose-pebbled bottoms,
And churned in the chilled and iridescent spawn
Of the crane's pool.
Clamped and flexed in the vise of her beating wings
Now flaring astride the brassy eye of the sun,
I gasped like a fish
Hung out in the harsh and sudden air
And flipped, past sparkling regions, underground.

JOHN LOGAN *grew up in Red Oak, Iowa, and was educated at Coe College and the University of Iowa. He has taught at Notre Dame University, St. Mary's College, and the University of Washington, is presently a Professor of English at the University of Buffalo. He is the founding editor of a magazine,* Chicago Choice, *and has published a number of short stories and three volumes of poetry —* A Cycle for Mother Cabrini, Ghosts of the Heart, *and* Spring of the Thief. *His work has been anthologized in English, Spanish, French and Italian, and has appeared in the leading periodicals, including* Poetry Magazine, Commonweal, Nation *and the* Kenyon, Partisan, Evergreen, *and* Sewanee *reviews.*

ELEGY FOR THE
REV. MR. JAMES B. HODGSON

I haven't talked to you since your death
but your picture still breathes
and flames in my dreams and at my eye.
I can tell you as a boy
folding back and back the loam
of your family's farm
as the beginning morning light grows like grain
in Wales or like wind blown fur
changes texture —
while your mother
turns again the pied
fields of quilts along the beds
and furiously sweeps your little room.
Or see you following the great, slow team
while you memorize the paradigms
of Greek
you pasted on the wooden wagon seat.

As a man you shepherded a white
Presbyterian Church, pointed and at rest,
a unicorn among the Iowa farms,
penned beside a field of marble colored blooms.

But I will surely not forget
that you also taught.
Small, lean body, annular face and eyes, metal rims
and a fixed (false teeth) grin
make up the picture
of my first beautiful teacher.
You taught us to listen to a book

like a lost, ancient father's talk,
and from the light in your eyes we knew
you
would become aroused
if a handsome library passed.
You gave me Goethe's *Faust* in German
and together we struggled over "time" in Bergson.
(Still for some instruction you weren't so strong —
walked away from a film on sex for the young.)
And you paid
the favorite praise to my poems when you, small eyes
        grey with peace, said
"You have experienced deeply both of nature and of
        grace."

I left the school, tried my young luck.
But I kept coming back
As if to beg someone's pardon.
Your wife made lunch in the garden
while you caressed the flower beds,
patting the dirt and pulling weeds —
or talked of your son studying abroad,
of your wife's portrait paintings on the wall,
and of your own apocalyptic book — undone until you
        would "retire
and have the time."
Twice I stayed the night.
But you would never break
reserve, and said at last,
"I shall follow your career with interest."

Sixty-five came, and you bought a tiny farm
where you turned
your father's earth over in your hand
and cherished close your aging wife.
But she gave up her life
the very first, quiet year,
and you would not stay there
by yourself, nor finish up your work.
Soon you too took sick
and died — with your mouth and cheek
all caved in like a hill of earth
under the heavy disc of a stroke,
unable to talk.

Still it isn't this I remembered on the afternoon
I learned your final lesson.
I was filled with an ancient image
seated on the stage
as you waited to speak at school.
You seemed to curl
forward into a ball;
your heavy head fell,
hands were born further down between the knees
as an infant is
before he leaves his early night.
You seemed to become more taut,
more formal
or compact, more integral.
And as the mass of your body bent,
and folded some, I saw it give off bright
streams as of language or light!

PAGAN SATURDAY

Hiking out to Ratcliff
School we took our shoes off
In the field of stubble
Where the graveyard ends; we ran
Shouting thru the stalks

Of pain that grow tipped
And colorful as grain.
We swarmed the woods and looked
For fun and fuel and packed enough
To pile and build to a roar

A very satisfying fire.
We set our mouths on hopes
Of stolen corn and raided
An easy field behind a barn;
And burst the milky kernels

On our thumbs. Letting
The fire at one side turn
To ask we buried our yellow
Catch inside its wraps of husk
And later, ate in heights

Of joy the cindered ears.
And racing along the rim
Of Indian Gully sudden
As fear light as laughter I felt
A creature flare with beauty

At the back of my eye;
I knew my limbs and body
Sang on me sometimes —
But this was brighter than my arms.
Coming back we played

Some rapid hide-and-seek
Among the graves; I hid
Awhile and searched the stone
Face for mother; and ran on
Into the pointed groves of pine.

LOVE POEM

Last night you would not come,
and you have been gone so long.
I yearn to find you in my aging, earthen arms
again (your alchemy can change my clay to skin).
I long to turn and watch again
from my half hidden place
the lost, beautiful slopes and fallings of your face,
the black, rich leaf of each eye lash,
fresh, beach brightened stones of your teeth.
I want to listen as you breathe yourself to sleep
(for by our human art we mime
the sleeper til we dream).
I want to smell the dark
herb gardens of your hair — touch the thin shock
that drifts over your high brow when
you rinse it clean,
for it is so fine.

I want to hear the light,
long wind of your sigh.
But again tonight I know you will not come.
I will never feel again
your gentle, sleeping calm
from which I took
so much strength, so much of my human heart.
Because the last time
I reached to you
as you sat upon the bed
and talked, you caught both my hands
in yours and crossed them gently on my breast.
I died mimicking the dead.

LINES FOR A YOUNG
MAN WHO TALKED

But I wish you would not hang your head.
It is that image lags inside my mind.
If you had known how much we need
to help our friend (Oh I think in some old
innocence perhaps you did)
you would not hang your head.
It was out of your own gentleness you cried
for aid. And it's not because I'm fond
of you (although I am) as if you were my son instead
of my young student and my young friend
that I do not want you to hang your head.
It is this: the bit you told —
no, not *what* but simply *that* you said —
was like a gift! An ancient gift of horses or of gold.

It was a grace. Oh I suppose you thought you had
    confessed.
But I am not a priest. To say you had been bad
and young and let you hang your head.
Use me to find in what way you are good.
Christ listen to your own charitable word!
We spoke so that you might understand
and be merciful to yourself. Here, give me your hand
for it is I who must feel ashamed
again, until you do not hang your head.

THE RESCUE

I doubt if you knew,
my two friends,
that day the tips
of the boat's white wings
trembled over the capped,
brilliant lake
and fireboats at the regatta
rocketed their giant streams
blue and white and green
in the sun just off the shore,
that I was dying there.

Young jets were play-
ing over the lake,
climbing and falling back
with a quick, metallic sheen
(weightless as I am
if I dream),

sound coming after the shine.
They rose and ran and
paused and almost touched
except for one
who seemed to hang in the air
as if from fear.

I doubt if you know,
my two beloved friends —
you with the furious black beard
your classical head
bobbing bodiless above the waves
like some just appearing god
or you, brown, lean, your bright
face also of another kind
disembodied
when you walked upon your hands —

That as you reached for me
(both) and helped my graying hulk
out of the lake
after I wandered out too far
and battered weak along the pier,
it was my self you hauled
back from my despair.

THOMAS McGRATH *was raised on a farm in
North Dakota, and studied at the state university there,
Louisiana State University and Oxford. He has been farm
and shipyard worker, freelance writer, teacher at various
colleges, and has written children's books —* Clouds *and*
The Beautiful Things *— a novel,* The Gates of Ivory, The

Gates of Horn, *and documentary films, in addition to the*
following volumes of verse: First Manifesto, The Dia-
lectics of Love (*in* Three Young Poets, *edited by Alan*
Swallow), To Walk a Crooked Mile, Longshot O'Leary's
Garland of Practical Poesie, A Witness to the Times,
Figures From a Double World, Letters to an Imaginary
Friend, *and* New and Selected Poems. *He has the dis-*
tinction of having made several of the better political
blacklists.

THE TOPOGRAPHY OF HISTORY

All cities are open in the hot season.
Northward or southward the summer gives out
Few telephone numbers but no one in our house sleeps.

Southward that river carries its flood
The dying winter, the spring's nostalgia:
Wisconsin's dead grass beached at Baton Rouge.
Carries the vegetable loves of the young blonde
Going for water by the dikes of Winetka or Louisville,
Carries its obscure music and its strange humour,
Its own disturbing life, its peculiar idea of movement.
Two thousand miles, moving from the secret north
It crowds the country apart: at last reaching
The lynch-dreaming, the demon-haunted, the murderous
        virgin South
Makes its own bargains and says change in its own fashion.
And where the Gulf choirs out its blue hosannas
Carries the drowned men's bones and its buried life:
It is an enormous bell,
        rung through the country's midnight.

Beyond the corrosive ironies of prairies,
Midnight savannas, open vowels of the flat country,
The moonstruck waters of the Kansas bays
Where the Dakotas bell and nuzzle at the north coast,
The nay-saying desolation where the mind is lost
In the mean acres and the wind comes down for a
      thousand miles
Smelling of the stars' high pastures, and speaking a
      strange language —

There is the direct action of mountains, a revolution,
A revelation in stone, the solid decrees of past history,
A soviet of language not yet cooled nor understood
      clearly:
The voices from underground, the granite vocables.
There shall that voice crying for justice be heard,
But the local colorist, broken on cliffs of laughter,
At the late dew point of pity collect only the irony of
      serene stars.

                          ❊   ❊   ❊

Here all questions are mooted. All battles joined.
            No one in our house sleeps.
And the Idealist hunting in the high latitudes of unreason,
By mummy rivers, on the open minds of curst lakes
Mirrors his permanent address; yet suffers from visions
Of spring break-up, the open river of history.
On this the Dreamer sweats in his sound-proof tower:
All towns are taken in the hot season.

How shall that Sentimentalist love the Mississippi?
His love is a trick of mirrors, his spit's abstraction,
Whose blood and guts are filing system for
A single index of the head or heart's statistics.

Living in one time, he shall have no history.
How shall he love change who lives in a static world?
His love is lost tomorrow between Memphis and
    the narrows of Vicksburg.

But kissed unconscious between Medicine Bow and
    Tombstone
He shall love at the precipice brink who would love these
    mountains.
Whom this land loves, shall be a holy wanderer,
The eyes burned slick with distances between
Kennebunkport and Denver, minted of transcience.
For him shall that river run in circles and
The Tetons seismically skipping to their ancient
    compelling music

Send embassies of young sierras to nibble from his hand.
His leaves familiar with the constant wind,
Give, then, the soils and waters to command.
Latitudinal desires scatter his seed,
And in political climates sprout new freedom.
But curst is the water-wingless foreigner from Boston,
Stumping the country as others no better have done,
Frightened of earthquake, aware of the rising waters,
Calling out "O Love, Love," but finding none.

THE ROADS INTO THE COUNTRY

Ran only in one direction, in childhood years —
Into mysterious counties, beyond the farm or the town,
Toward the parish of desire the roads led up or down
Past a thicket of charms, a river of wishing hours,

Till, wrapt in a plenum of undying sun
We heard the tick of air-guns on the hills.
The pheasant stalked by on his gilded heels,
The soft-eyed foxes from the woods looked on,

While hung upon the blue wall of the air
The hawk stared down into a sea of fire,
Where, salamanders in our element,
We ate the summer like a sacrament.

That was another country, and is lost.
The roads lead nowhere. Aloof in his field of fire
The hawk wheels pitiless. Alone, afar,
The skirmishes of childhood hurry past,

Hunting a future that they cannot will.
Children of light, travelling our darkened years
We cannot warn them. Distant, they have no ears
For those they will become. Across a wall

Of terror and innocence we hear the voice,
The air-gun in the land of mock-choice;
Around us not the game of fox and pheasant,
But the gunfire of the real and terrible present.

THE TROUBLE WITH THE TIMES
for Naomi Replansky

In this town the shops are all the same:
Bread, bullets, the usual flowers
Are sold but no one — no one, no one
Has a shop for angels,

No one sells orchid bread, no one
A silver bullet to kill a king.

No one in this town has heard
Of fox-fire rosaries — instead
They have catechisms of filthy shirts,
And their god goes by on crutches
In the stench of exhaust fumes and dirty stories.

No one is opening — even on credit —
A shop for the replacement of lost years.
No one sells treasure maps. No one
Retails a poem at so much per love.

No. It is necessary
To go down to the river where the bums at evening
Assemble their histories like cancelled stamps.
There you may find, perhaps, the purple
Weather, for nothing; the blue
Apples, free; the reddest
Antelope, coming down to drink at the river,
Given away.

ESCAPE

Hunting in the dark my father found me,
My mother claimed me, and led me into light,
From my nine-month winter. In the herds of Right,
Branded and bawling, the christeners bound me.
God given, church shriven, hell washed away,
Adam purged, heaven urged, the dog would have his day.

Hell all about me with its infantry
Storming the fortresses of my crying years
Could not get my notice. They had stopped my ears
With chrism of love in my infancy.
World poor, world pure, I kept my head level,
Unproud, but uncowed, shaming the devil.

And thus betrayed I fell into a world
Where love lives only in another name.
At eleven or twelve, when the kidnappers came,
I took the poisoned candy and off we whirled.
Innocence, nonsense, the seven priestly lies
Surrounded me, when, hands bound, I opened my eyes

Onto the bloody barnyard of my youth
Where the stuck pig wetly squealed against the wall,
And fell on the stone crop. False, rich, tall,
The elders judged me. The stone edge of truth,
Flint-sharp, heartless, stabbed my begging knee —
Harmed me but armed me: I cut my hands free.

THE BUFFALO COAT

I see him moving, in his legendary fleece,
Between the superhighway and an Algonquin stone axe;
Between the wild tribes, in their lost heat,
And the dark blizzard of my Grandfather's coat;
Cold with the outdoor cold caught in the curls,
Smelling of the world before the poll tax.

And between the new macadam and the Scalp Act
They got him by the short hair; had him clipped
Who once was wild — and all five senses wild —

Printing the wild with his hoof's inflated script
Before the times was money in the bank,
Before it was a crime to be so mild.

But history is a fact, and moves on feet
Sharper than his, toward wallows deeper than.
And the myth that covered all his moving parts,
Grandfather's time had turned into a coat;
And what kept warm then, in the true world's cold
Is old and cold in a world his death began.

POEM

I don't belong in this century — who does?
In my time, summer came someplace in June —
The cutbanks blazing with roses, the birds brazen, and
    the astonished
Pastures frisking with young calves . . .
                That was in the country —
I don't mean *another* country, I mean in the *country*:
And the country is lost. I don't mean just lost to *me*,
Nor in the way of metaphorical loss — it's lost that way
    too —
No; nor in no sort of special case: I mean
Lost.

Now, down below, in the fire and stench, the city
Is building its shell: elaborate levels of emptiness
Like some sea-animal building toward its extinction.
And the citizens, unserious and full of virtue,
Are hunting for bread, or money, or a prayer,
And I behold them, and this season of man, without love.

If it were not a joke, it would be proper to laugh.
— Curious how that rat's nest holds together —
Distracting . . .
                    Without it there might be, still,
The gold wheel and the silver, the sun and the moon,
The season's ancient assurance under the unstable stars
Our fiery companions
                    And trees, perhaps, and the sound
Of the wild and living water hurrying out of the hills.
Without these, I have you for my talisman:
Sun, moon, the four seasons,
The true voice of the mountains. Now be
(The city revolving in its empty shell,
The night moving in from the East)
— Be thou these things.

THE NEWS AROUND MIDNIGHT

Past midnight now, and the city in its first heavy slumber
Lies on its right side.
                    The stars ride forth.
                                        The last
Quarter of the south-hung moon bars the skies with its
      light.
Cold light there for a fact and the late and empty streets
Cold in their dark and lack.
                    Now, on the hill, my window
Is a star, no farther. And still, in this Here, I spin my luck,
I work my light . . .
                    here at the table with the formica top

As the despairing generations dream toward the day
Which can only be tomorrow, I prepare my spells and
 tools.

There is a planter here with a bit of green in it —
A cutting of Impatience which has just begun to root,
Some Mother-in-Law's Tongue, and a green shoot of
Leucojum just showing through — though I was a wild-
 rose man,
A Tiger Lily and Sassafras and Gooseberry man,
A man for the hill-hurdling crow calls and the cries of the
 killdeer
Falling through the green burden of the Autumn
 sundown woods.
But these are my tools now. These and my lonesome
 ghosts,
And the endless echoes of want in the lost streets of the
 terrible city.

Many nights you may see me here, around about
 midnight,
If you should look.
                    Below me the city turns on its left
Side and the neon blinks in a code I can all too clearly
Read. It will go down with all hands.
                                     Meanwhile
The moon steers and the stars wheel steady in the
 ultimate North.
The ghosts sing round my light. Far in Dakota now
My father is dying. And here, in the silent house, in
 shadowy

Rooms lying, my wife and children in their perfect sleep
Explore a darkness I can never reach.
Necessary recorder.
                    A voice.
                            This sad machine —
It does little good, I know; still I am here —
This sad machine: for love.

AH . . . TO THE VILLAGES!

Leaving the splendid plaza and the esplanade —
The majestic façades of metropolitan unease —
Let us to the vast savannahs of despair
Repair; and let us seek
The panoramas of malaise, the continental anguish,
The hysteria and the nausea of the villages.

Somewhere — perhaps where Omaha, like a disease,
And the magnificent, brumal names of Fargo, of
        Kalamazoo,
Infect the spirit with magnificent ennui —
A baroque splendor attends our small distress:
We dress in the grand extravaganza of cafard.

Still, there will come evenings without true
        discontent —
The sparrows loud in the dust and the crows gone
        cawing home
To the little wood; the lights ending at the prairie,
        and —
As the divine and healing night comes down —
The town reeling with unreasonable content.

In the one-horse town they have eaten the horse — allons!
But soft! Here are not only the megrims of small forms
And the subliminal melancholy of the central square.
Take care; for here you find
An intermontane anguish in the wind that sings you
    home:
Here is a false front distinguished as your own.

And contentment is momentary in the villages.

PARM MAYER *was born in Michigan and has lived
there all his life. He has degrees from Olivet College and
the University of Michigan, and presently teaches at
Northwood Institute in Alma. He is an associate editor
of the Michigan periodical* Voices. *The Spring 1966 issue
of* Epoch *included him in its list of "The Top Fifty Living
American Poets," and he has appeared in over forty
literary journals, including* Antioch Review, Beloit Poetry
Journal, Chicago Review, Colorado Quarterly, Kenyon
Review, Midwest, Minnesota Review, Northwest Review,
Prairie Schooner, Shenandoah, Southwest Review, *and*
Western Poetry Journal.

THE NIGHT FREIDA TOOK MY
SPIRIT BY SURPRISE

Sometimes it was on a wooden porch steps
on a farm in southern Michigan,
under the jewelry of the stars, let us say,
So you'll know something of what I'm surveying.

And she was harvestful
as a fieldful of ripened grain;
full-moon breasts; vine-ripened lips;
abundant buttocks you knew were there
but couldn't see.
One of those few who eat your poetry
without first fingering it.

I knew at once that here was someone
who would not continually analyze
the tick-tock of my themes;
could orient my paradigms
if I lay them out before her;
would not sweep down
my spiderweb of thought.

This is not Paris, I said,
and we are not sitting on a bank of the Seine.

She said, Your spool of hope is unwound;
imagination has overslept and there is
the wormwork of nagging thoughts.

Neither is it Budapest; or even Hong Kong,
I reminded. But a wooden porch steps
of a farmhouse in southern Michigan.

She said, the body's made to hold but one;
my bed is big enough for two.

That is all I am going to tell you.

Sometime, you may discover for yourself
how sweeping an unexpected pounce can be,
even when you are trying to brace yourself
against the charming pitfalls
of the night.

THE DAY I LAY MYSELF DOWN

There were the knotted cries
I had not heard in the beginning
and the soft impact
of watered-down requiem;
the whacking of bone against bone,
and a cave-cold dripping
in what was left of hell.

There was the long waiting,
like starers at a rose-bowl parade;
hoping perhaps to catch a glimpse of heaven,
though faked and full of earth.
And there was Death,
toothless and tattered (but still lively)
walking through a town
he has learned to call by name.

I said, Ha!
And reminded myself
to rebel against the green fog
of my cultural heritage;
to fight for a way to preserve

the continuity of dangerous change;
to search for fulfillment
of chaste and muted dream.

But there was Earth,
standing with its mouth open,
eyeing me like a tiger who is no longer
ashamed of eating flesh.

So I sent
a bouquet of black roses
to the first contingent of mourners,
and proclaimed:
Life is more than can be included
in a single volume.
And there is little evidence
that it is wise to turn everything
over to God.

I said, Ha!
And wrapped myself in a box
of newly-sawed silence,
exactly my size.

I EAT A SLICE OF BREAD

I cut myself a slice
of just-baked bread
(saw saw saw and then
the sound of knife on board)
and sit down at the empty

kitchen table and eat it,
bite by fervent bite, sensing perhaps
some sort of original intention
to perpetuate myself.

No butter. But tooth to tooth
with succulence of what
is close to earth:
a field of ripened grain,
alive with sun and wind.

I smack, but no one here
to lift an eye. But
I am not alone; for I
am one with you and you and you
who sit and eat with no disguise,
not pretending life is wholly good.

` I do not laugh. (My joy
is a slow-baked soft-crust kind.)
I feel my calloused hands
and know the satisfaction comes
from the bonework process
by which the bread was earned.

I say to myself:
        There is no solution
        to a million dollars.
        And why should I
        infuriate myself
        by contending with kings.

PLEA TO A PARTICULAR
SOFT-HANDED GODDESS

Where there are no streets
the world is less remembered,
and hypotheses are lean and scattered.

I kneel before a pine-tree-standing;
listen to the locust-singing of my soul;
hope for a brimful of some sort.

I pray for raindrop ablution;
for embodiment of sandhill dreams;
for a scheme to end

this bughouse commotion;
these spasms of faddism.
The question is:

How to work out a pardonable truce
between one's honest opinion
and the official attitude.

What I really want is for you
to come and stand beside me
and probe with pagan tenderness

Beyond my bone-weight
until you find a forgotten disclosure
like the surprise of my being.

EPITAPH FOR A
LITTLE-KNOWN GRAVESTONE

Summer me a song
along a road where rivers run
and miles are out in front
in green. And corn is quiet
in the stalk. And trees
are fragrant pattern on a hill.
Let clouds perform their last charades
in country sky.

Textured fruit: my mind
all brown and yellow vined.
And what once melted into Spring
is brushed by wind
and hung to dry.

Never again
edge to edge with what
is bitter hung and willow ragged
on strange trees. But wrapped
in layers of a little known
and silent world.

How can they say
the Earth was spinning night,
when all along
it was the morning
my head was new!

REVIEW OF THIS
MORNING'S GRAVEYARD

With nothing to defend,
you lie in your interlude of darkness;
sealed in sullen chambers
where no doors swing
and no sound enters —
witnesses to the wastefulness of God.

I suppose
it's something new at first;
something to look at
with your glasses on.
Until you wake up
and find your veins clogged;
your mouth stapled.
And you feel you'll be
more than ever carrion,
come another spring.

Beneath my feet
your bones take shape and you become:
a conjugate good-night kiss;
a mouthful of go-to-hell;
a blue veil of shyness,
abandoned on a wedding night.

You, still have your mustache on;
were once sure-faced and muscle-boned,
and not attacked by alarms
that race up the spine at night.

Now, there is
a flickering of pale aghast;
a yellow shadow of resignation.

And *you,* I can see,
were once loud-looking
and sweetly nibbled at, no doubt.
Gave the boys
something red to remember;
something to make them laugh
and slap their thighs fiercely
in a fling of raucous night.
What happened
to bleed the flame from your lips;
quiet the shape of your breasts;
clamp your legs coldly together?

And *you,* who looked like Jesus
asking questions in the temple;
why are you still weeping
as though you stepped across
a velvet rope you shouldn't have.

And *you,* old man,
who hung himself on Christmas Day.
Who didn't want no Bible words;
no flower smell; no fancy-satin bone box;
no damn lid slammed down on your face.
Who broke a milk stool on a cow
and ran a pitchfork through a cat.
Who spoke unspeakable words
with furious pleasure.

Who scrupulously avoided
ordinary escapes from life.
Who twice sent egg money to C-A-R-E,
care of local postmaster.

I said to me:
Go home and explore
various kinds of death;
take off your clothes
and strike yourself with fire.

With a new-kindled sense
of negotiation,
I demanded the absolute
of the marble Redeemer
who stood beside me
in this absence of excitement:

Can the dead ever recover!

ON A WHITE BEACH

This could be
the playground of young gods,
I said. This breeze
which has gathered up the thoughts
of one more generation of waves;
the ethos of this sand,
which portrays the one sure basis
of my understanding;
these cries of water birds,
fluttering between the vernacular
and the syllables
of a tidal philosophy.

Why then, is the moon reluctant
to add meaning to what could be
a festival approach;
an eremite,
who has lost connection
with social factors?

Except for a few devout adherents,
the benches are abandoned.
And some, who were here yesterday,
walk arm in arm,
not knowing they are bone.

How can I resolve
the drift of my days;
the dead-fish dissolution
of my dreams?

To those who haunt
this improbable beach,
I say quietly:
I could not be God;
I could not bear to see
so many drown.

AFTER SHOOTING A COCK PHEASANT LAST FRIDAY

How desperately you rose
to escape the focus
of my mindless call to HALT;
only to be toppled

by the funneled force
of 1¼ oz. of speeding no. 6 shot.
Wing shattered by the tricks I play,
you lay, shorn of the weapons
of your ancestors; head up,
eyes on me and on what
was sure to be a losing pitch
for charity.

Stupefied by my astonishing role,
and with no God to guard me
from the peculiar pride
that crowed in the late afternoon
of my mind,
I clutched your mortal plumage,
fearful I still might lose
the chunk of victory
I had torn from the sky;
soon to bulge against my back,
pocketed so in hunting coat:
tail feathers extending congratulations
and offering some kind of tall corn
we call status.

Now you lie, coldly feathered
on my basement floor;
doomed head still wondering
why you took to the slaughterhouse
of the air, when you could have
just as well cursed me
from the ground.

With the embarrassing sound
of an accident occurring too soon,
I rip off skin and feathers;

not noting your reaction
to lying there nude
on yesterday's Saginaw News.
No explanation, either,
for wounding your plumed pride.

Like a butcher
wearing a contradictory face,
I knife off: wing tips, spurred feet,
pronged tail, white-ringed neck and head —
anything that is not appropriate
to your ghost.
Make a shambles of your bowels;
tear still-warm heart and lungs
from their coveted positions;
spill corn and weed seeds from your craw;
slit gizzard with no apology
for the madness of the process —
as if I was cannibal as well as conqueror
and still might expose
a cluster of savage laugh.

As yet, no feasting nose
conjuring you prepared (chicken-fried)
for the graveyard of my maw;
but a red fingering
of the day's real feast:
a letter to my son in Ludington,
closing casually with a line
I'd been trying to say for five years:
Got a pheasant today,
just before dark. One shot.

LISEL MUELLER *was born in Germany but educated in the United States. She holds a bachelor's degree in sociology from Evansville College and has studied folklore and social work in the graduate schools of Indiana University and Loyola University of Chicago. She now lives in Lake Forest, Illinois.* Dependencies, *her first volume, appeared in 1965, and her work has been published in various anthologies, including* Best Poems of 1958, *and many periodicals, among them* Poetry Magazine, The New Yorker, Saturday Review, Sewanee Review *and* Perspective.

FIRST SNOW IN LAKE COUNTY

All night it fell around us
as if the sky had been sheared,
its fleece dropping forever
past our windows, until our room
was as chaste and sheltered
as Ursula's, where she lay
and dreamed herself in heaven:
and in the morning we saw
that the vision had held, looked out
on such a sight as we wish for
all our lives:
a thing, place, time
untouched and uncorrupted,
the world before we were here.

Even the wind held its peace.

And already, as our eyes
hung on, hung on, we longed
to make that patience bear
our tracks, already our daughter
put on her boots and screamed,
and the dog jumped with the joy
of splashing the white with yellow
and digging through the snow
to the scents and sounds below.

ROOKERY: BROOKFIELD ZOO

One came forth
from the jumble of beaks and feathers
and flew past the towering lights,
his outsize keepers,
into the lawless dark

and came back singing,
unsteady with the delight
of having discovered danger,
the secret garden,

and tumbling above the crowd
shrilled his incredible tidings
over and over, as if
those grounded ears could hear,
those soft bellies rise.

A GRACKLE OBSERVED

Watching the black grackle
come out of the gray shade
into the sun, I am dazzled
by an unsuspected sheen,
yellow, purple, and green,
where the comb of light silkens
unspectacular wings –
until he, unaware
of what he means at this one
peculiar angle of sun,
hops back to his modest dark
and leaves the shining part
of himself behind, as though
brightness must outgrow
its fluttering worldly dress
and enter the mind outright
as vision, as pure light.

ON FINDING A BIRD'S BONES IN THE WOODS

Even Einstein, gazing
at the slender ribs of the world,
examining and praising
the cool and tranquil core
under the boil and burning
of faith and metaphor –
even he, unlearning
the bag and baggage of notion,

must have kept some shred
in which to clothe that shape,
as we, who cannot escape
imagination, swaddle
this tiny world of bone
in all that we have known
of sound and motion.

CICADAS

Always in unison, they are
the rapt voice of silence,

so singleminded I cannot tell
if the sound is rich or thin,

cannot tell even if it is sound,
the high, sustained note

which gives to a summer field
involved with the sun at noon

a stillness as palpable
as smoke and mildew,

know only: when they are gone
one scrubbed autumn day

after the clean sweep
of the bright, acrid season,

what remains is a clearing of rest,
of balance and attention

but not the second skin,
hot and close, of silence.

"THE EXPENSE OF SPIRIT IN A WASTE OF SHAME"

Two-tone motels and unlit lovers' lanes,
the usual drinks, the stale, expected lines,
standard persuasions of the lips and hands,
the motions of delight, and all the time
the laughter of some demon in his ears.
Something is wrong: he blames the hour, the place,
forgetting he has been love's whipping boy
since rose-point fans were used as barricades,
before an age of women whose legs show
and who will answer simply yes or no.

To the lost dreamers, kissing in the woods
of their own legend, miracles are not new;
but he, bedroom agnostic, cannot see
with the clairvoyance of the faithful, who
blow on the spirit with the body's breath
and by that doubtless summoning of light
make good their heat. Shy of the test by fire,
he haunts the outskirts of the wilderness,
where charms, unblessed, are futile; in his brain
the tired demon sighs, *try try again.*

FIGURE FOR A LANDSCAPE

Look, the solitary walker
out on this coldest Sunday of the year
shoulders the whole burden of the fable
which winter is, the moral panorama
of a silence so vast that all sounds have meaning.

In summer the landscape was simply
itself, and concealment humanly possible
in grass and shadow and the living noise
of child singers and animal dancers,
baroque in their cultivation of opulence

and the green life. But now
even the lake is petrified out of sound,
and the sky, impartially plundered
of inessential leaves, birds, clouds,
throws back his face without kindly distortion

as though he alone could answer for winter.
The tracks of the dead and the dying accost him,
crossing his footprints wherever he walks,
stands, is alive; and the clamor of ice
comes down with a crash, like an unstruck bell,

splitting his ears. In this season,
while we stay home with coffee and morning
newspapers, sensible of the danger
confronting us in the sight of a branch
gloved by a child's lost mitten,

he is the hero who bears all loss,
who, by no particular virtue
other than solitude, takes on himself
the full silence, the whole terrible
knowledge the landscape no longer conceals.

THE POWER OF MUSIC
TO DISTURB

A humid night. Mad June bugs dash themselves
against a window they should know is there;
I hear an owl awaking in the woods
behind our house, and wonder if it shakes
sleep from its eyes and lets its talons play,
stretch and retract, rehearsing for the kill —
and on the radio the music drives
toward death by love, for love, because of love
like some black wave that cannot break itself.

It is music that luxuriates
in the impossibilities of love
and rides frustration till two ghosts become
alive again, aware of how the end
of every act of love is separateness;
raw, ruthless lovers, desperate enough
to bank on the absurdity of death
for royal consummation, permanence
of feeling, having, knowing, holding on.

My God, he was a devil of a man
who wrote this music so voluptuous
it sucks me in with possibilities
of sense and soul, of pity and desire
which place and time make ludicrous: I sit
across from you here in our living room
with chairs and books and red geraniums
and ordinary lamplight on the floor
after an ordinary day of love.

How can disaster be so beautiful?
I range the beaches of our lucid world
against that flood, trying to think about
our child upstairs, asleep with her light on
to keep her from vague evils; about us
whose loving has become so natural
that it has rid itself of teeth and claws,
implements for the lovers new at love,
whose jitters goad them into drawing blood.

But o my love, I cannot beat it back,
neither the sound nor what the sound lets loose;
the opulence of agony drowns out
the hard, dry smack of death against the glass
and batters down the sea walls of my mind,
and I am pulled to levels below light
where easy ways of love are meaningless
and creatures feel their way along the dark
by shock of ecstasy and heat of pain.

JOHN F. NIMS *grew up in the midwest and received a doctorate in Comparative Literature from the University of Chicago. He has been a Fulbright Professor in Italy and a Visiting Professor in Spain, and has done well-received translations from the poetry of both countries. Presently he is a Professor of English at the University of Illinois (Chicago Circle), and often teaches at writers' conferences. His work was included in* Five Young American Poets, *and he has published three volumes of verse — The Iron Pastoral, A Fountain in Kentucky, and Knowledge of the Evening. He has*

translated St. John of the Cross and Euripides, among
other great writers, and served as an associate editor of
The Poem Itself. His edition of Arthur Golding's Meta-
morphoses of Ovid appeared in 1965. He has been on
the editorial staff of Poetry *Magazine for several years,*
and in 1960-61 was its Visiting Editor.

MIDWEST

Indiana: no blustering summit or coarse gorge;
No flora lurid as disaster-flares;
No great vacuities where tourists gape
Nor mountains hoarding their height like millionaires.
More delicate: the ten-foot knolls
Give flavor of hill to Indiana souls.

Topography is perfect, curio-size;
Deft as landscape in museum cases.
What is beautiful is friendly and underfoot,
Not flaunted like theater curtains in our faces.
No peak or jungle obscures the blue sky;
Our land rides smoothly in the softest eye.

Man is the prominent fauna of our state.
Elsewhere circus creatures stomp and leer
With heads like crags or clumps. But delirious nature
Once in a lucid interval sobering here
Left (repenting her extravagant plan)
Conspicuous on our fields the shadow of man.

PENNY ARCADE

This pale and dusty palace under the El
The ragged bankers of one coin frequent,
Beggars of joy, and in a box of glass
Control the destiny of some bright event.
Men black and bitter shuffle, grin like boys,
Recovering Christmas and elaborate toys.

The clerk controls the air gun's poodle puff
Or briefly the blue excalibur of a Colt,
Sweeps alien raiders from a painted sky,
And sees supreme the tin flotilla bolt.
Hard lightning in his eye, the hero smiles,
Steady MacArthur of the doodad isles.

The trucker arrogant for his Sunday gal
Clouts the machine, is clocked as "Superman!"
The stunted negro makes the mauler whirl
Toy iron limbs; his wizen features plan
The lunge of Louis, or, no longer black,
Send to the Pampas battering Firpo back.

Some for a penny in the slot of love
Fondle the bosom of aluminum whores,
Through hollow eye of lenses dryly suck
Beatitude of blondes and fallen drawers.
For this Cithaeron wailed and Tempe sighed,
David was doomed, and young Actaeon died.

Who gather here will never move the stars,
Give law to nations, track the atom down.
For lack of love or vitamins or cash
All the red robins of their year have gone.
Here heaven ticks: the weariest tramp can buy
Glass mansions in the juke-seraphic sky.

POOLROOM

When children's day is over and nurses lay
Their little kelsons in a feathery port,
With chromium tooth and fluorine-scarlet lip
Grins open now the emporium of sport.
Carefree in earnest, sombre women bowl,
And highschool fry are loud in many a shoal.

Through blue narcotic fog, tables of game
Swim undulant to the golden eye of beer,
Standing like wharves, and in their sunken deck
The colored mice collide and flee in fear
As some to their ultimate Thule clicked and tossed
Plunge in the purple bayou, fathoms lost.

Things of all color on the table live:
The nineball is a bronze eel in the moss;
The luminous three like a flamingo flies
In the green sky forever, and still across
The ivory garden rolls the shadow of fate:
That midnight ambulance, the sable eight.

Stricter than merchants of a hard bazaar
The rubber euclids in the cushion lie,
In sinai-flash their forks of anger deal
Law to all orbits of that carom sky.
The elegant brow their bitter lightnings vex.
Darkie or drunk is subtler haruspex.

The players lean; the tiny balls like bass
Swim mimic in the mirror of each eye.
Hither we drift from oaths of love or pain,
Forgetting the wings and tracers of the sky,
Forgetting what cueball follows, shaped like a train,
Or a Packard shipwrecked on the curbs of rain.

MOVIE

Making a stately crossword of the night
New stars are rising, *Gem* and *Regent*. Soon
Great *Tivoli* takes the heaven, rose and white,
Blanching Orion and the dappled moon.
Around the roof supreme auroras flow:
Performing fire and circuses of snow.

Nor fade to common on the brightest day:
Fanatic murals daubed with sex and joke
Along the wall delirous sagas lay,
Amassing miracle for a simple folk
That to this haunted pit as palmers wend,
Offer their mite and bid the god descend.

Within, the faces in their peanut choir
Hang luminous, row on row, like the pale dead.
Sign of burnt children and disastrous fire
The stars of exit brood, forever red,
While dance in spearmint heavens of flu and dust
The sleek mirages of the moon of lust.

These fluoroscope the anatomy of dream:
High breast and brow, long limb, pellucid lung;
No fish of sin milting in any stream;
Love's motor instant and forever young.
No blade or blackest fracture in this ray;
Never the stain that eats the face away.

Buried, we age like moles, a pasty clan
From rays of morning and frank shadow fled,
Making the sadbright centuries of man
A gape and snicker in a rented shed.
Our saints: the bawd and fatso. In fake night
They mince and quiver in the choirs of light.

ELEVATED

Three stories up the town is Venice: there
The streets' abrupt and windy rivers run
Among the badland brick, the domes of tar,
The mica prairie wheeling in the sun.
On crags of glass the sooty lichen twine;
Flowers of the wash in highland vineyards shine.

Along the banks of tile and metal mushroom
The orange liners of the transit ply.
From bunks of plush the mariners behold
The hollow maelstrom with indifferent eye.
Serene to wreck, they loll and even read,
Their schooner reeling in a sea of speed.

The green pagoda, floating in the tree,
Honors the pauper and the drunk buffoon,
Slow negroes too (the negatives of men)
Wearing their midnight faces even at noon.
All come and throw, like dice, the copper fare,
Win ships of glass and navigate the air.

Master the changes of all weather too:
When steeples quaver in the August glow
Or windows in wet April spin like reels
Or when the track's a portico of snow.
Mostly at rung Noël, the frozen star
Hears all night long the heaven-skating car.

We float an eerie deep, as men that mark
The fabulous water in a keel of glass;
Beneath the bay of rippling window, loom
The tenant's cave and honeycomb crevasse —
Queer grots of mossy rug, crustacea pan,
Framing the sad and seahorse shape of man.

On nights of rain, the captain in the prow
Dares in great dark the iron-charted flood,
Follows a star of harbor green as mint,
Skirting disaster's little eye of blood.

Is fortunate yet, for sudden in the night
Stations arrive like Indias of light.

Exotic foliage on the wooden shore
Fertile with ads: tobacco, rouge, and coke
Finer than flora swarm. Have proper care
From censoring pigeon, friend to lonely folk.
Here girls in jest or desperate or tight
(Like votive wax) their phone and hungers write.

What dreamer hung the hollow sky with ore?
No Merlin he, or caliph in a tale.
Some ne'er-do-well, some boy who liked to draw
Blueprinted first the levitating rail.
Rubbed a right lamp, and saw, when that was done,
A crowded city moving in the sun.

The crazy dream is record and charts time,
Gables the region with a frieze of steel.
Saturn is peeled of credit, on whose ring
Never the flash and thunder of such wheel,
Where no batons of hard momentum flail
Music of acrid iron from the rail.

As princes, wrecked and ragged, long pursued,
Show in some tone the grandeurs of their birth,
So we, who fever on a foreign bed,
Who beg for lust and moulder in sad earth,
Greatness remember, and with viking eye
Storm the ancestral headlands of the sky.

FOR DAPHNE AT CHRISTMAS

Christmas again. And the kings. And the camels that
Travel like shanties collapsing. We hurl
Fistfuls of shivery bliss in the night on a
Tree that runs fall-color, breathes of a girl.

Men had a myth: how Apollo (no kin of mine)
Flushing in shrubs a bent shoulder and head,
Snorted and plunged for her, lofty blood
thundering —
"Oh," she said. "*Oh!*" she said. There's a girl sped.

Hovered high hurdles; flashed a fine knee or so,
Flashed a fine — Ovid says, how her flounce flew.
Cornered, she crinkled to armfuls of laurel, her
Heartbeat in bark ebbing. Likely: I knew

Much the same story: once scuffled fall foliage;
Caught the soft runaway, crushed to my brow
Curls that turned holly-leaves, pin-pointy, hissing
things;
Felt the warm bark alive. Heaven knows how

These had gone walking all the broad autumn,
Poked in gold cubby-holes down the dark run;
Fumbled in foliage crisp as old tinsel, and
Tussled and scuffed too much. Blurting: "Been
fun."

Fun? — but it wasn't fun. Blundered half purposely
   Into each other — through wool such delight?
     "I want you all," he choked, "cornflower, corntassel!"
     "Oh," she laughed, redder then. *"Oh!"* she wept,
     white.

"Snug rough and tumble here? Fun in a furrow bunk?
   What would you do, gamin? Turn to a tree?"
     "I don't know." Tears flickered. "I don't know."
     Hems flinging.
     Whitely defiant though: "Try. And you'll see."

Down the dense calendar's black and red stubble field
   Gone, the October girl. Plunging, he kept
     Eyes on a — cypress? Dead mistletoe? Myrtle-bush?
     Oak that had crashed on him? Willow that wept?

Ashen as sassafras? Judas-tree? Juniper?
   Trekking November, he scuffed the dull days.
     Pinned her at Christmas, in cedar gloom wassailing.
     Sombre, and swirling dark rum as she sways:

"What's a gone girl to you? Better: forever things.
   All the fall-forest bit; all the dense kiss.
     Look, I'm a tree." She spun tasselled with tinsel, and
     Pinned, in her pony-tail, tree-glitter: "This

Crimson for lips, the fall foliage ranting;
   Gold for that foliage blurred the wind's bliss.
     Blue, for dense gloom in the cornstubble starlight;
     Silver — for lashes lay salt to the kiss.

Better a tree. So embrace me, I'll do for you."
   Arms like boughs bending, she downed the dark rum.
      "Better a year-spirit. Others have summer. But
         Mine, when the kings and the camel-train come."

THE ACADEMY DISPORTING

In love with shadows all our days,
Creepers shunning dark and bright:
The dutiful, who troop to gaze
On friendship's long-exhausted rite;
To fob and shuffle palm to palm
Coppers of accustomed thought:
Decades have tested all we say;
And we lope roguish, as they taught.

Beneath the mistletoe will drift
Kisses the flat "punch" half warms.
Wan mirage of kisses. No
Likelihood of thunderstorms.
Compilers would look far to find
Milder perversities of lust.
There is no ruby in this ash:
Kisses that half stir the dust.

White shoulders we would press today —
Time is a great page torn between!
We nibble polite watercress
Fresher than memory, more green
Than Junes which gloated-over here

Would blast the many-eyebrowed room,
Alarming almost to its feet
The tableau stable as a tomb.

From where the soul with level look
Is hinting its contempt too well,
We flee — who cannot be alone —
Like bats poured panicky from hell.
From where the eye we dare not meet
Burns ruby in immortal bronze,
We break and run like giggling kids —
Ecstatic if a portal clangs.

Is there no lightning in the land
To show us, bitter black and white,
The car, the cottage, and the dune,
The hound a-howling all that night,
And where the imprudent, hand in hand,
Sway naked in immortal surf?
What vision haunts the summer land?
What wound is closing in the turf?

Shrimp on little picks impaled
Lie naked to the decent eye,
Grey frost their bed. Our fingers lift,
Insert them goggling, and put by —
Quashing a thunder in the soul
That rages to make all things right:
In love with shadows all our days,
Creepers shunning dark and bright.

MARY OLIVER *was born in Maple Heights, Ohio, and attended the state university and Vassar College, after which she lived in New York City for a few years. She then stayed in England for about a year and a half, during which time* No Voyage and Other Poems *(1963) was published. After her return to this country an enlarged book of the same title was brought out (1965). She belongs to the Poetry Society of America, which in 1963 awarded first prize in its annual contest to the title poem of her book. Publishing regularly in the periodicals, she is at work on a new volume, and presently lives in Provincetown, Massachusetts.*

A POEM FOR HOME

We spread across the table
The wrinkled maps of earth
To find out where we are.
Four thousand miles away,
Size of a pin, I touch
The leaves, the wicked towns,
The dry hills of my birth.

Four thousand miles away
I walk beside the sea,
And learn another grammar,
And look for news from home, —
As if Ohio weather,
Where sin lies parched for rain,
Had meaning, still, for me.

All hillsides thick with leaves
Wait to cast their spell.
Ohio is my name,
Whose blue and yellow springs,
Whose hard unchristian land
Crawl through my spirit like
Caught oceans in a shell.

Child of those dying hills,
Nations from where they stand,
I pray there will be rain,
Rain, till the earth grows fair
As when I learned to care,
As when I learned to bear
That first imperfect land.

NO VOYAGE

I wake earlier, now that the birds have come
And sing in the unfailing trees.
On a cot by an open window
I lie like land used up, while spring unfolds.

Now of all voyagers I remember, who among them
Did not board ship with grief among their maps? —
Till it seemed men never go somewhere, they only
      leave
Wherever they are, when the dying begins.

For myself, I find my wanting life
Implores no novelty and no disguise of distance;
Where, in what country, might I put down these
      thoughts,
Who still am citizen of this fallen city?

On a cot by an open window, I lie and remember
While the birds in the trees sing of the circle of time.
Let the dying go on, and let me, if I can,
Inherit from disaster before I move.

O, I go to see the great ships ride from harbor,
And my wounds leap with impatience; yet I turn back
To sort the weeping ruins of my house:
Here or nowhere I will make peace with the fact.

BEYOND THE SNOW BELT

Over the local stations, one by one,
Announcers list disasters like dark poems
That always happen in the skull of winter.
But once again the storm has passed us by:
Lovely and moderate, the snow lies down
While shouting children hurry back to play,
And scarved and smiling citizens once more
Sweep down their easy paths of pride and welcome.

And what else might we do? Let us be truthful.
Two counties north the storm has taken lives.
Two counties north, to us, is far away, —
A land of trees, a wing upon a map,
A wild place never visited, — so we
Forget with ease each far mortality.

Peacefully from our frozen yards we watch
Our children running on the mild white hills.
This is the landscape that we understand, —
And till the principle of things takes root,
How shall examples move us from our calm?
I do not say that it is not a fault.
I only say, except as we have loved,
All news arrives as from a distant land.

HOW I WENT TRUANT FROM SCHOOL TO VISIT A RIVER

There was a small river ran by our town.
It ran unguessed south by the setting sun:
Snake with green wings, it took all forest with it.
Birds sat and laughed upon the townward thickets;
Fox was a scarlet blink along its shores.

When school bells rang, I crept the echoing halls,
Slipped like a needle out of doors, and ran.
So sly! Like colt I leaped in a blond gambol.
But wonder warmed my cleverness to sleep,
And I went ferreting as any scholar

Where fish like nails with rainbows on their sides
Mulled in pools and herons dipped and poised;
Where feral berries glistened under thorns,
Where green leaves sighed the grammar of their hour
And bloodroot bloomed like alabaster verbs.

Noon stroked the sparrow's head with a windless thumb;
His mathematics drifted down the air.
The far bells tolled; I watched the wing's clapped drama;
I lolled beside the fine geometry
Of blue and wet-legged herons turned to stone.

Ah, still the dead bells sing, of some Pericles
Barefoot once along some marvelous river,
Of herons and the calm bird-havening trees,
In strophes like waterfalls, through the otherwise
Muttering ruins enclosing the dust of a child.

DANCERS AT BANSTEAD

I went inside the place to find
The madmen dancing in the hall,
The witless women whirling by
Like phantoms, trailing scarves and smiles;
A little band, with lips of tin,
Kept puffing out the ancient cry:
To dance! To dance! To happiness! —
And round they went, without a pause.

At midnight when I drove away,
And back to dreams the madfolk went
Tucked in to sleep with lullaby,
I flung my questions to the air.
But nothing cared to answer me:
The dark hills humped down everywhere
With matted arms; and over all,
Full-blown and white, the neutral moon
Was dancing to another tune.

Ahead I saw the city's lights
And thought, if earth can only wait
Another thousand thousand nights,
Surely this grief will balance out
In some unguessed nativity.
Meanwhile, indeed, the nights are long,
And there is little we can do,
Except to let the dancers dance;
Except to know the moon is wrong.

A LETTER FROM HOME

She sends me news of bluejays, frost,
Of stars and now the harvest moon
That rides above the stricken hills.
Lightly, she speaks of cold, of pain,
And lists what is already lost.
Here where my life seems hard and slow,
I read of glowing melons piled
Beside the door, and baskets filled
With fennel, rosemary and dill,
While all she could not gather in
Or hide in leaves, grows black and falls.
Here where my life seems hard and strange,
I read her wild excitement when
Stars climb, frost comes, and bluejays sing.
The broken years will make no change
Upon her wise and whirling heart; —
She knows how people always plan
To live their lives, and never do.
She will not tell me if she cries.

I touch the crosses by her name;
I fold the pages as I rise,
And tip the envelope, from which
Drift scraps of borage, woodbine, rue.

AFTER MY GRANDFATHER'S DEATH:
A POEM OF THE CHINA CLOCK

The china clock, for all her winding of it with a curious
    key,
Stand still,
Or moves whimsically, —
Not really trying to catch up, not really trying at all,
But now and then announcing one filigree hand on
    twelve:
Small golden blows upon a hidden bell.

My grandmother wakes at seven o'clock by the sun;
Small and shawled, light as a last year's twig,
She tilts across the gardens.
At seven-thirty, by the sun,
She is clucking for chickens in an empty barn,
Hunting for cows in an empty meadow.

When the sun reaches noon of the sky
Hunger and habit combine to bring her home,
And the question of things not found
Contrives, amid news of sparrows and roses,
Once more for a likelier answer;

And we who are all abandoned now,
We who sit sane and sad, with the wrong reply,
Lean on among the plates and the bread.
                          But silence

Even to children, it is said,
Has meaning.
                    And my grandmother then,
My own, my truly lost one,

Out of the cloth of this one almost returns;
Almost there is nothing to divert her then from finding
That refused burden:
The thing she would not know; —

When from a far room, chiming sweet as salvation
And calling her back to the vague figurine smile,
The clock cries out: I have moved!
                                    It is the hour
Of some rose and sparrow-decorated day
Some few unreasonable, ungathered years ago.

ANTON AND YARO

Sifting among the photographs, like leaves,
Now for the hundredth time, the old man smiles
And plucks my arm. I know that he has found
His gray-eyed brothers poised in the new orchard.
The others, aunts and uncles, drift haphazard
Back to the teakwood box. Happy, we stare
Down sixty years into an April morning.
Huge-shouldered, burly, with their brown trimmed
          beards,
Yaro at nineteen, Anton, twenty-two,
Shake their brother's hand and say goodbye.

They have helped set the Baldwins in the blue
Ohio earth, the tender waving sticks
That tower now above our patient summers.
Rumors of prairies wide as the Atlantic
And mountains choked with gold shake in their dreams.
Now for a few years news will come of them
Out of the prairies, from some mountain town;
And then a final postcard from the ocean.
We cannot read it. Time has rubbed away
All but the coiled springs of their signatures.

Here in his kingdom of trees and daughters,
My grandfather bends to his eighty years,
Grows drowsy in a small and closing circle.
Outside the house, the weathers rise and drift
Beyond our knowledge, where the clouds are hammered
Into the shapes of horses, gods and dreams.
I watch them, from the warm room, sink beneath
Wind and the final hills. The sun is setting;

The old man sleeps. I rise and leave the house,
Walk to the trees and listen to the wind.
Slowly I gather in the fallen apples,
And earth lies cool and pure beneath my knees.
I know the gray-eyed brothers have not failed,
For there are islands flung through the Pacific
And there are plains beyond the tossing sea.
Across Ohio, now, the night draws in.
Swept to the house by dusk and sudden love,
I pause before the door and look, once more,
And in the blue light almost think I see them, —
Two bent white giants striding through the trees.

Down every street the uncles cluck their tongues;
The aunts are sharp as birds, but I keep silent.
I do not doubt they will at last come home.
Wide is the earth, and stranger than its legends; —
They will come back. My thoughts range outwards now
Beyond the leaves, under the hammered clouds
Towards hills and towns ten thousand miles away.
My dreams begin to shake with radiance;
The golden mountains cast a second spell.

And yet I fear to think of things so far.
I remember how the gray-eyed brothers
Climbed from this windy place and disappeared.
When they come back to us, then we shall know,
Shall see our lives like crosses on a map
Of landscapes strange and manifold as morning;
Then we shall stand, on that white edge of day,
And stare upon the hills and hammered clouds, —
And fear shall be like night, that blows away.

ELDER OLSON *grew up in Chicago and was edu-
cated at the University of Chicago, where he presently
teaches. His books of poetry are* Thing of Sorrow, The
Cock of Heaven, The Scarecrow Christ, Plays and Poems,
and, in 1963, Collected Poems. *He has also written a
number of critical volumes, among them* The Poetry of
Dylan Thomas *and* Tragedy and the Theory of Drama.
*He received in 1935 The Friends of Literature Award,
in 1953, the Eunice Tietjens Memorial Award, and in
1954 the Poetry Society of America Award. His work has
appeared in important anthologies and in most of the
leading literary quarterlies.*

WINTER NIGHTFALL

January hangs glowing glass
Icicles at eaves and sills.
Day lifts past broken blinds and chimneys.
But high west-spaces glitter yet
And cast such influence beyond night
That folk blaze in the brilliant cold,
And beggars shuffle astral snows;
The cur at street's end, shivering, chill,
Burns in as pure furious light
As stars or absolute Beings wear,
But sniffs a dazzling refuse still.

Now all's of such proud metal wrought
That lost amid excess of light
The body shivers, not for cold,
But for the vision, winter-bright,
Of radiance bone nor flesh had dulled,
And but a season's penance bought:
Prison and slum and market-square,
As if their substance were but shade,
Glimmer and grow unreal and fade;
The winter lights mount, tier on tier,
As ringed saints on the transpiring stair.

Now the high heavens are like a bell
Repeating peal on peal of light,
But, O, in counterfeit largesse:
These fires though fallen from heaven's height
Will keep no mortal fabric warm,
Nor are of godly gaze begot,
For that divinity is blind

That cannot look on worser things,
But makes all exquisite to its eyes;
Godhead must enter and inform
The sorry shape with Paradise.

And once, they say, it happened so,
But now that wizard's tale is told.
It too ends in mortality
And what the mortal is, we know.
Though all the heavens compound their fires,
The shades of night close round again
Like these returning prison-walls,
And though the Child but lately born
Yet fills with radiance all the west,
He perishes at the fall of dusk;
And at the street's end, the dusk falls.

JACK-IN-THE-BOX

Devil sprang from box,
Frightening the children, who would not be comforted.
In vain they were wooed with all the other toys;
Expecting new terror, they would not look or listen; like
    an angry demon
Their fear ran round the house, from room to room.
At last their mother led them off to bed.

Allison lit his pipe; forgot it, thinking.
Something more had been released
Than long-necked Punch, nodding and leering still.
As in the ancient casuistry of Eden,
Falsehood, accepted, falsified all truth;
All the old pleasant facts now fell away,

Flimsy as Christmas wrappings; there was the house,
   now,
Pretty with snows, with candy roofs and sills,
Sparkling and false as the hut in the fairy tale;
As if in a haunted forest shone the tree,
With fruits — pear, apple, plum — poison-bright.
Outside the wind swept away the Christmas illusion, in
   a white fog
Where toys like Martians stalked, destroying all.

He thought: how simply terror can enter a house.
The angel, treed, was trembling, that had promised
   peace.

PLOT IMPROBABLE,
CHARACTER UNSYMPATHETIC

I was born in a bad slum
Where no one had to die
To show his skeleton.
The wind came through the walls,
A three-legged rat and I
Fought all day for swill.
My father was crazed, my mother cruel,
My brothers chopped the stairs for fuel,
I tumbled my sisters in a broken bed
And jiggled them till all were dead.
Then I ran away and lived with my lice
On my wits, a knife, and a pair of dice,
Slept like a rat in the river reeds,
Got converted fifty times
To fifty different creeds

For bowls of mission broth,
Till I killed the grocer and his wife
With a stove-poker and a butcher-knife.
The mayor said, Hang him high,
The merchants said, He won't buy or sell,
The bishop said, He won't pay to pray.
They flung me into a jail,
But I, I broke out,
Beat my bars to a bell,
Ran all around the town
Dingling my sweet bell,
And the mayor wanted it for his hall,
The merchants wanted to buy it,
The bishop wanted it for his church,
But I broke my bell in two,
Of one half a huge bullet made,
Of the other an enormous gun,
Took all the people of all the world
And rolled them into one,
And when the World went by
With a monocle in his eye,
With a silk hat on his head,
Took aim and shot him dead.

THE NIGHT THERE WAS
DANCING IN THE STREETS

More paper blackened with more signatures;
Top-hats and handshakes, smiles of dry-toothed
        diplomats;
Crowds, drums, flags, cannon, fireworks, torchlight
        processions.

Truce, peace, alliance,
What matter, what matter?
    Close the windows, now,
Light the lamp, and read Thucydides

Who knew that passion and character of a nation
Stemmed from far causes; poverty of the soil
Brought safety; safety, growth, eventual greatness;
Habit of growth, ambition; the quick Athenian
Was his own land's best harvest, and so flourished.
Conversely, now richness of earth brought war,
Stunting increase, and the sullen Spartan
Sank man in soldier; the armor molded the man.
Thus power and fear of power grew side by side,
Contrary blossoms out of contrary earths;
There lay the principles of war; meanwhile, let run,
Let rhetors roar and heralds strut, let town
Quibble with town; the tough root turns all axes,
The fruits of Necessity ripen in all weathers.

THE MIDNIGHT MEDITATION

I

Midnight: I pluck the curtains back, look out
Into a city clouding, silently sinking,
Falling away, fading, engulfed in gloom.

Already ruinous! — the last catastrophe
And final nightfall visibly at hand;
And the wind, now, the wind around a ruin,
Or the wild sea-race through the long sea-halls.

O semblance desolation, seeming is truth:
The city of yesterday that here goes down
Is gone forever, like sunk Lyonesse;

Gone forever as Babylon or Troy
Or towns faint-glimmering that profoundly lie
Drowned in the depths of endless centuries.

II
Immensity, like the darkness cast from the cloud above
And the darkness earth-born, I am lost in you
Deep as profound towns buried in Time.

I have no mind to mourn with a mournful season,
Mock-mourning of the autumn leaves, of the keening
      wind,
All savage rites kept by the ancient earth.

I mourn, not grieving, no, at grievous death,
But at the resurgence after death,
And the death again, and senseless resurgence still.

Cycle on cycle, wheeling Infinity,
Boundless Abyss where all things rise and fall,
You are my sickness: the terror of which I dream, and to
      which I awake.

Nightmare phoenix ceaselessly renewed,
Riddling sphinx indifferent to all response,
Paradoxical chimera guarding chaos,

How have you not betrayed us in our journeys,
As the simple immensity of sombre wastes
Turns the lost traveller in a circling track.

Infinity, patient and silent as a beast following,
How subtly have you stalked us in all travels:
Indeed, wherever we went, we were yours at last:

— You, with bones of empires in your craw,
Swallower of whole civilizations, and dainty yet,
Scrupulous still, to capture a lone traveller.

III
Let children ride the year's sweet carrousel,
Glitter of revolving winter and spring;
We know that faëry wheel and where it takes us.

The illuminated heavens, promising enchantment
Like powerful symbols in a magician's book,
Reveal at last a single simple meaning.

In infinite Time the cities burst like rockets, empires
    gleam and are gone,
The bright seas run like quicksilver,
The mountains rear and recede with the waves' motion.

Cloudy Time obscures, yet dulls not so
But fragments of our history survive
To mark how all our action was but motion,
Wind's course, flame's thrust, turnings of the whirlpool.

Patriot, scholar, poet, soldier, saint,
Nothing will eventuate from your anguish:
All faiths and arts are figures on a wheel.

Nothing will come of all these revolutions:
Agonies of the liberator
Prepare new tyranny for new overthrow.

The straight line returns upon itself.
Is infinite, too: all contraries are one.

IV

I thought once I should have at a man's age
Some wisdom hard and pure as diamond
To make the center of a new steadfast world,

Or some bauble, at least, for a toy — accurate enough
To catch the universe in its gay reflex,
Like Paris reflected in a jewel,

And perhaps after all I have it: at last recognizing
The treadmill as a treadmill: asking of my empty
        journeys
Nothing, in the end, but to spare my private nobility;

Dwelling at last in a house on the cloudy brink
Where the windows offer no prospect,
And the balconies give on nothing;

Knowing that though we speak with our old sophistry
Of the dawn of hope, the dawn comes endlessly,
Day after trailing day, but our hope never;

As now the new day comes, with its new horrors
Still inert, its tyrannies still voiceless,
And the future rises, like these light-dripping towers,

Like a city rising from the infinite sea.

RAYMOND ROSELIEP *is a priest of the arch-diocese of Dubuque and has taught at Loras College for the past twenty years.* His three books are The Linen Bands, The Small Rain, *and, in 1965,* Love Makes the Air Light. *His poems have appeared in more than a hundred periodicals, including* Poetry Magazine, The Nation, Modern Age, Prairie Schooner *and the* Minnesota, Chicago, Massachusetts, Georgia, *and* Literary *reviews. He has given poetry readings at universities and has recorded poems for the collection in the Lamont Library at Harvard University.*

VENDOR

On the New York Central from Chicago to South Bend
I saw him — at first from the back — and mistook him for
the conductor. His uniform was weary and dark,
his railroad cap might have come off the ark, and his shirt
collar was officially white under the stone grey.
On his tin tray he carried among the gimmicks some
cracker jack & tomato juice (and I had to wince
after cataloging them in files of Innocence
& Experience). He rattled up and down the aisle
of our coach a mystical 7 times — I counted.
Of his visagë children were aferd, very few
asking their mothers for a dime or two. Flesh sagging
from the bonework of his face and neck was the color
of frost bitten corn, his eyes had unhappy people
in them, and his drained lips crackled. The hands I had
      seen
Before, on Halloween or in a home doctor-book

a boy will sneak through. He was hunched, rickety. And
    true.
(Little use to bury my head in Wolfe's epic of
the Angel — I strayed away from that confessional,
unable to put my ear by the stick crossed window
and help a man/boy say his fable.) The vendor held
me: I could feel him as a poem or candle-end.
So I was rather glad when we pulled into South Bend.
That night I took a cold shower and tried to send him
down the drain. I had enough ghosts of my own for bed-
fellows anyway, and would prefer sleeping with *them*.
But I didn't. I kept buying cans of tomato
juice which I poured into half filled waterpots of gin,
telling him a half truth about my fountain of youth.
When he wouldn't even wet his dryleaf mouth, I bought
a hundred boxes of his cracker jack, and I strung
the sticky kernels on christmas cord, though not too loose.
Round his neck I looped the noose, and hung him on a
    hook
in the skyblue ceiling of the 7th coach where kids
whispered innocent transgressions into the latticed
ear of a priest (whose wooden face never seemed to care
what else was toppling in their parish). Then I cried out
to them with a loud voice, and they came wide eyed and
    stared.
Before I died, I dangled till my skin burned to husk.
The grinning bones were left uncoffined. In single file
those children passed, the vendor leading them up the
    aisle.

WAYS OF MY EXILE

Exsilii mei vias tu notasti . . .
PSALM 55

November goes dryfooted and is bare this midyear
in my wandering. A changing of the breath, switching
of the eyes' angle, and I puff the afternoon air,
strain to see each calendar of my unmanly grief
flutter as the fashionable leaf in the act of falling.

The winesap in the cheek of that boy punting
his football over the telephone wires, the curly
haired legs ardent with his nineteen summers, the torso
lank as a new linden, the arms a rise of killdeers:
he is the seed springing out of due time and season.

From her porch, the girl watching is younger by a year,
and her hair is musk melon tinted, her skin rivals
the last huddling marigold in its picket prison;
her body is tendril, floating, tenuous, brief in
the antique afternoon of my journeying; she clings
to the boy. She loves him: and is a light forgotten.

On the dry earth under the deadleaf street, the boy drop-
kicks the ball: the air cracks and it hums with the stinging
in the thighs of my older life.
                        A few wet flakes touch,
now spatter the naked flesh of ground. Night is at hand:
the air grows articulate, entering some bough, and
the ways of my exile lengthen the vowels of snow.

November is no land for lovers. So I will pull
my collar tight around my throat, spend a final glance
on the girl whose name I know, wave
only once, and show the boy tenderly to my grave.

GREEN BEDROOM

I painted my bachelor bedroom green; drapery,
spread, rug, also post-pentecostal, drum the mono-
tone. My friends smile, and a few even groan heavily.
This is where I sleep alone, dream not always alone;
and I haven't paged a book of Freud to discover
what the leaf & stem, for instance, meant to that lover
Narcissus, accounted only a white flowerhead
by most of us. Green-for-hope is a cliché facile
as light, and I know the undertow of my mind will
never pull the wholly jocund or liturgical
when moving within the decor (more private than sin).
Though I do go down to the shore for explanation.
Gliding silently as Huckleberry when night has
begun, I enter the mothering sea where the broom
of wind had been busy, and I creep along the vault,
diamonded with olive eyes the old mariner
blesses far under the aegis of his peculiar
moon, slip by toy-broken shell shapes in the cave
      windings
where the mermaids do not hide and pearls cobble the
      floor,
and the child man neither toils nor spins for his living,
whose love is a girl's name faded on a sunken ship,
lily quiet, and the formal water all over

is louring as a naked christmas tree, and I leap
softer than Shelley's moth for the star
into the elemental, small suicide of sleep.

TIRED EQUINOX

My boxer with brindle coat and I
go out to trail spring. Unlike the dog
at the heels of young Tobias, mine

runs the hills ahead of me, and why
not when there is no angel to bog
down our climbing into the dayshine.

I whistle what bird notes I capture,
meadowlark, redwing, vireo, thrush,
and my dog picks up his unfooled ears.

Growing impatient at my rapture
over a flaming violet's plush
feel (like a sudden body), he clears

the air of my drifting when he barks
at a treetop where no squirrel dwells;
and I go to view his pretending.

Both pretenders, we lose our footmarks
on these ever lasting hills,
and I ease into fleshweary spring.

HUMMINGBIRD

my gold and coral tubes of
sugar water bring
down

from his spiderthread
saliva
woven nest

of lichen
and plant
down

sleight of
hand celestial
helicopter lander

unlanded
suspending
motion

backward
trapezing
I'm dizzy

ruby throated
and no
longer see

HOSPITAL VISIT

It seemed strange going
down Locust Street picking
up autumn leaves in early August
and storing them like
grain in my pocket bin

to bring you. Though long ago
you were used to my ways,
my mother with the steel
pin in your hipbone
slight as a willow whistle.

Float them on
the linen locking
your body
in the manner of
light soil

or dandelion
down;
label them after sun-
sets
you call from a too west window

before you trim
your table as a tree;
ring a ring of them around
ceramic Francis
with his grounded bird;

jump as a
child or poet
wild on the crutch of
belief in the rained-
down, colored leaf.

TOUR. IN RAIN

No weather can unbrother brothers. Rain
was putting signature on street and town.
Over the route that waves us otherwise
apart I came to you, drawn by the late
rain. My eyes called out and were answered:
the wet cement returned your body inch
by inch, distorted in the sickly yel-
low flow of lamps on corners like a faith;
and I was quick to feel the terrible
unfolding of your man's life in an hour
or night which gave the emptiness its power.
I cried, not as a man cries for what is lost,
rather for what is hardly found on the
dull and sudden ground.
                              I followed, and
imagined fallow land, the desert place
you said you would not die in, or the dry
white wine a priest will trickle on his fast.
But you were given to the rain that night
and could not hear a footstep crackle sharp
as Mass wheat in your falling street.

HEELS WEAR DOWN

Michigan Blvd. at 6:00 is risk-
y, but he left the walk to hail a cab,
and sparks undid the cold november curb.

Too much Picasso had me swaying, and
I shivered as we rode to catch a drink
"somewhere within an English otherworld"
because he liked a far-off atmosphere.

Pineapple soaking in a rum, the almond,
and the never bitter raisin sauce
pampered the tongue, and we talked poetry,
and were not ashamed as men: outrun-
ning beauty and without a frequent soul
to bargain with.

              I thought it rather strange,
however, he should be annoyed that I
had sermonized how stars came from his shoes
and broke the night. He found a deeper vein
beneath my careless parable than I
had counted on.
              "Just cleats," he said, "my heels
wear down too fast." He had the master's knack
of flattening with words.
              "And so does ale —
shrimp curry — and the spirit" (now I felt
my way into the homily).

"Let's not
have God tonight." He dulled my pulpit plan.
Then looked at me and spoke with louder eyes
than voices from Picasso.
                              Paid the check.

And hailed another cab which brought us to
a public reading of his poems: not
so bright as sparks that briefly warmed or died
along the curb.

MY FATHER'S TRUNK

The soft grainy light of our attic opened
my father's past a little way. His trunk was
a place where years were shut in him like the leaves
of a book whose title alone he displayed
— I wondered if it was mostly about love,
though other strengths were there pressing a vision
on my landscape. I loved the hunters riding
in coontail caps through the ornamental path
inside the lid — I knew by heart the clipping
how he bagged a timber wolf in some woods near
Farley, Iowa, and I sported the brass
knuckles and dangled the billyclub of his
sheriff days, I aimed the elegant pistol
at spider targets — the topmost color in my
first spectrum was the greenpearl of the handle.
Under the sulphur whiteshirts with hard collars
and their beautiful musty smell and the old
leather smell of razorstrop were keys to locks

I never could open; an oval locket,
sealed tight as a dream, carried I always thought
my mother's image. I tried never to laugh
at the ohio matchbox with the sewing
kit of his bachelor days, and though it was
hard to picture the big fingers threading a
needle, I once saw that hand lift a bluebell
from its tower and twirl it like a sparkler.
The letter in the blue envelope he had
never opened bore a script daintier than
my mother's exquisite flourish, and when I
left the blue flap sealed, ordinary breathing
avowed the silence but did not disturb it.
Stale flower smell on another clipping brushed
me like rain: "a knot of English violets
enhanced the heliotrope gown" his bride wore
at their winter wedding, before "a long tour."
And every solitary honeymoon
to the attic filled my boyhood for a while.

One day I heard the plunk-plunk from our chestnut
tree, the gang all pocketing them for our pipes,
small fry on the block playing stickball, the flash
and thrust of limbs. I sat cross-legged before my
father's trunk and the wilderness of myself.
Signs I found in the tenacious silence of
things: I was the black-footed ferret, juggler,
harlequin: I was a touch on the padded
stairs, a balance of milkweed seed, Picasso
performance. With this strange fine figure of man
I had been playing follow the arrow and
capture the flag. Outside, someone was calling

ollie-ollie-oxen-free, and I was free
as a robin, a sun print on a swimmer,
the detached brownleaf and the unfallen snow.
Slyboots of that giant of my childhood, built
so long of limb and entangled in those dark
lidded privacies, I was equidistant
to 'love that makes the air light.' Chip of his strength.

DENNIS SCHMITZ *was born in Dubuque, Iowa,
and schooled at Loras College and the University of
Chicago. His poems have appeared in many leading
periodicals, including* Hudson Review, Prairie Schooner,
Southern Review, Minnesota Review, Chicago Review,
and Choice. *He has taught at the University of Wisconsin
in Milwaukee, presently teaches at Sacramento State
College.*

THE RESCUE

I

we came to the portage at sundown
I had promised them lawns
but the grass came
yellow & stale like the inside
of a bear's mouth. the trees shook
down fruits which we ate
being voyagers,
exiles. apples tough as spools

& the dark heels of wild
plums we trimmed in our hands
while the juice worked into the blisters
& we ate our own pain.

Peter was sick, so we left most
of our gear twenty miles
back in a tree, the tins in the sack
like a wind-bell high
in a black fork where the jays
sink down rippling
their throats in anger & I see

the shadows stirring the scum
around the willows
after us. no waves, only the faint
wingbeat
of the water as it settles.

II
we will rest here for the night
only. Jack & I caught
for a few hours in another's body,
the close underbrush, briars:
a wilderness we dreamed of our own
bodies. the moon trails

up a dark fir, the highest. we are
in the big trees: firs,
spruce & scrub fire-growth
underneath.
the colorless tendrils seeking

the tap-roots of the bigger
trees toppling
them by fractions as we die
more in the wet seasons from one
another's growth. we stay
away from Peter, the fine beat
of his nostrils like the leaves

turning over before a storm.

III

we didn't hope for a town:
rooms, some way of dividing the silence,
walls we could give
ourselves to. not parlors bound
in rich papers, but even rough boards
with unchanging knots
we could study. on still days
I thought I could hear the brief sigh
of a flushed toilet. we hoped
to see a trail or the red
gleam of slightly-rusted rails
in the gravel-beds. but the meadows

gave out again to the trees.
we stopped more often &
one day after
a swim, I crawled away downstream
ashamed, at last only sure
of myself. I masturbated in the bushes
on my knees to some vision
of origins. the beasts cried out
in the woods around me. birds broke

away from the water.

IV
the gift of tongues
unfortunate that man keeps
so many words & the animals
knowing few, work out a closer

meaning. a coon
& a small one stand by a still
pool as we pass
farther out in the stream
straining to pull the canoe
past each paddle-
stroke while they silently enjoy
the threshold, sifting
the air for the foreign goal

we seek & they know the forest
will repeat as it has
given trees & the same substance
to the leaves for generations.

the flies feed undisturbed
on Peter's face, singing
fervently to the febrile blood
that rises in blue
patches to his cheeks. promise
of the deeper pools
under the bone
lintels where the veins crawl

more slowly now.

V

the yellow canvased
plane of the ranger, the propeller
snoring through the gold
coins of the sun it throws
down. we signal

we are here, to those above
that we have suffered
the lonely ocean of green
life. have gone over the heart
with our own rib-
bones like a rake, palms
against our chests afraid to speak
to animals & the stones

that stare up
under our stopped canoe. the ranger
above flaps his wings though
he hasn't heard over the roar
of his own going nor seen the small

forms his fellow takes. Jack
says he will be back &
perhaps another boat upstream
will descend to gather
up the sick & those of us who
remain, paddles trailing
in the water, to the last tasting
perhaps knowing, too late. yes,
I said to Jack, yes he will.

THE FISHING

the leaves were knee-
deep
around the elms &
inside the stream
the fish
flashed like spears
at the feathers
of the hook
dreaming of birds.
on the bank in the solid
air
the rod looked
like a spear in the sun.
overhead a hawk
lay on top the air
like a leaf
　　lifted up by the stream.

IT IS THE KEY

to the river that
takes root
in the trees shaking

　　　the birds from its shoulders
breaks
the sun on its anvils

we die also
by hammer-blows
inside the heart

will be tempered by water
watch

the water in two
months will no longer tremble
like fine tin
sheets

one thin
willow leaf locks
the river in ice

THE RABBIT LEAVES

the rabbit leaves
a track
like two dry fingers
in the new snow
the new season! & I have put
my fingers
once to a dying rabbit's
guts
that wound like roads
between the bones
where the bung-hole opens
on the white fur
like an eye

THE WOUNDED DOE

steps out of the green
& yellow handsful
of leaves still on the trees
her soft ears

tremble like butterflies

berries are crushed
against her coat
&
her wet breath crumbles
white
on her muzzle

all the bones of her body
are braced
against her teeth

& I am so close

I can hear the slow
fingers of her blood working
away from her skull
as her death
drains into her body

& she waits to fall

BEFORE THE COMING
OF WINTER

I counted the shapes
of my face on the dying
leaves

& was never cheated

choose my body too
empty the trees
onto their shadows

I want to be lean & tough
as a fir
& float across the snow
in green
like an enormous flame

KARL SHAPIRO *was born in Baltimore, Maryland,*
and attended the University of Virginia and Johns
Hopkins University, yet for many years he has been
strongly associated with the midwest and has cham-
pioned its poetry. In 1946 he was made Consultant in
Poetry at the Library of Congress and in 1947 joined
the faculty of Johns Hopkins. In 1950 he became editor
of Poetry *Magazine, a post he held for a number of*
years. He then began teaching at the University of
Nebraska, where he served as an editor of the Prairie
Schooner. *Presently he is a Professor of English at the*
University of Illinois (Chicago Circle). His second vol-

ume of verse, V-Letter and Other Poems, *was awarded the Pulitzer Prize in 1945. Other books are* Person, Place and Thing; Essay on Rime; Trial of a Poet; Poems: 1940-1953; Beyond Criticism; Poems of a Jew; In Defence of Ignorance; *and* The Bourgeois Poet, *from which the following selections have been made.*

7

The bourgeois poet closes the door of his study and lights his pipe. Why am I in this box, he says to himself (although it is exactly as he planned). The bourgeois poet sits down at his inoffensive desk — a door with legs, a door turned table — and almost approves the careful disarray of books, papers, magazines and such artifacts as thumbtacks. The bourgeois poet is already out of matches and gets up. It is too early in the morning for any definite emotion and the B.P. smokes. It is beautiful in the midlands: green fields and tawny fields, sorghum the color of red morocco bindings, distant new neighborhoods, cleanly and treeless, and the Veterans Hospital fronted with a shimmering Indian Summer tree. The Beep feels seasonal, placid as a melon, neat as a child's football lying under the tree, waiting for whose hands to pick it up.

14

The password of the twentieth century: Communications (as if we had to invent them). Animals and cannibals have communications; birds and bees and

even a few human creatures, called artists (generally
held to be insane). But the bulk of humanity had to
invent Communications. The Romans had the best
roads in the world, but had nothing to communicate
over them except other Romans. Americans have con-
quered world-time and world-space and chat with
the four corners of the earth at breakfast and have
nothing to communicate except other Americans. The
Russians communicate other Russians to the moon.
The entire solar system is in the hands of cartoonists.

I am sitting in the kitchen in Nebraska and watching a
shrouded woman amble down the market in Karachi.
She is going to get her morning smallpox shot. It's cold
and mental love they want: It's the mystic sexuality
of Communications. Money was love. Power was love.
Communications now are love. Sex-object of the tele-
phone, let's kiss. The girl hugs the hi-fi speaker to her
belly: it pours into her openings like gravy. In the
spring, Hitler arises. This is the time of trampling.
My japanned birds in the radioactive snow are calling.

A man appears at the corner of the street; I prepare my-
self for hospitality. Man or angel, welcome! But I am
afraid and double-lock the door. On the occasion of the
death of a political party, I send an epitaph by West-
ern Union. I didn't go to the funeral of poetry. I stayed
home and watched it on television. Moon in the bottom
of the Steuben glass, sun nesting in New Mexican
deserts — the primitive Christian communicated with a
dirty big toe. He drew a fish in the dust.

#18

One of those idle autumn evenings on a street as harm-
less as an Eskimo Pie, the young ones chatter on the
porch with their aunt, a woman of intelligence, as they
say. Someone across the street has died some days ago.
Once in a while a long wail of a female voice, as
though from a quite distant bedroom. It is somber and
full of dread, yet only a phrase, a Berlioz tune. We
discuss it thoroughly, how it trespasses on the music
of the street. And the aunt, taking the side of the
young perhaps, would quieten such grief, cure it more
quickly, have it get up and bathe and fill its lungs with
air and look at the world, though different now, but
still the only world.

Spoken too soon. Another week and her husband dies, a
man of reputation, in excellent health. Something has
drawn me to her porch again: the family is coming
from the cemetery. They carry her from the car; her
screams rip through the harmless street. Others are
running from others cars. By the end of the day half of
her face is turned in paralysis. For months her mouth
lies in a twist — that grief that parodies a smile.

#27

Why poetry small and cramped, why poetry starved and
mean, thin-lipped and sunken-cheeked? Why these
pams, these narrow-shouldered negatives? (The best
we can say is that they're seed catalogs.) And why

those staring eyes, so carefully fixed on the photographic plate? Why no lips at all but in their stead the practiced line of anger and the clamped jaw? Why always the darkening halo, so seemingly satanic? (The best we can say is that they are trying to mirror our lives. Do they know our lives? Can they read past the symbols of our trade?) Why so much attention to the printed page, why the cosmetology of font and rule, meters laid on like fingernail enamel? Why these lisping indentations, Spanish question marks upside down? Why the attractive packaging of stanza? Those cartons so pretty, shall I open them up? Why the un-American-activity of the sonnet? Why must grown people listen to rhyme? How much longer the polite applause, the tickle in the throat?

What will fatten you, skinny little book? What will put lead in your pencil? All of you dust-collecting seed catalogs, to the Goodwill you go, to the broad stench of the paper mill! Seed catalog, go pulp yourself!

Poems, flowers of language, if that's what you are, grow up in the air where books come true. And you, thin packet, let your seed fly, if you have any.

2 9

The living rooms of my neighbors are like beauty parlors, like night-club powder rooms, like international airport first-class lounges. The bathrooms of my neighbors are like love nests — Dufy prints, black Kleenex, furry towels, toilets so highly bred they fill and fall without a sigh (why is there no bidet in so-clean America?). The kitchens of my neighbors are like cars: what gleaming dials, what toothy enamels, engines that click and purr, idling the hours away. The basements of my neighbors are like kitchens; you could eat off the floor. Look at the furnace, spotless as a breakfront, standing alone, prize piece, the god of the household.

But I'm no different. I arrange my books with a view to their appearance. Some highbrow titles are prominently displayed. The desk in my study is carefully littered; after some thought I hang a diploma on the wall only to take it down again. I sit at the window where I can be seen. What do my neighbors think of me — I hope they think of me. I fix the light to hit the books. I lean some rows one way, some rows another.

A man's house is his stage. Others walk on to play their bit parts. Now and again a soliloquy, a birth, an adultery.

The bars of my neighbors are various, ranging from none at all to the nearly professional, leather stools, automatic coolers, a naked painting, a spittoon for show. The businessman, the air-force captain, the professor with tenure — it's a neighborhood with a sky.

4 1

Not at all my favorite author, Kipling described Chicago
once: the water is the water of the Hooghly, and the
air is dirt. And as famous a poet of New England
whom I drive to the station: it's a grand city. (*Grand*,
a nineteenth-century word.)

Under its permanent umbrella of travail, Chicago swirls
in grit. Smuts drift in the sky, penetrate window glass,
light on petals of window-box flowers, turning gera-
niums pansy-black. All is charred, all is furred with
dirt, the sky winter and summer streaked like the sky-
light of the grandest railroad station, basilicas of prac-
tical kings.

But now we take leave forever by car, driving in early
morning south, miraculously out from under the soiled
umbrella, south and more south in the dead blue
winter light, south and west in the snow-light, till the
snow rots in Arkansas, then west again, the holy di-
rection.

Far from the Chicago cave, spring comes facing toward
summer, such summer as happens only in one place in
a given country.

There is a rise (where is it on the map?), on one side
America and on the other, California. There you look
down on promised advertisements of green come true,
green for the eating, money-green, and the rows of the
royal palm for welcome, official, frightening. The Cali-

fornians live in California. The money groves are green. America is a suburb of California et cetera et cetera.

America is Hooghly.

5 4

Mr. Cochran flags the train. One man with a flag can stop all that steam and steel and make it roll again. He sits in a doll house by the railroad track and we go there to keep him company. All day he whittles and tells us stories. He whittles us fine sticks with designs. His favorite pattern is pitting with an awl. A stick of wood becomes a talisman with stars, indentations, smooth and magical. When we go home for our nap we show our treasures.

Two Boy Scouts climb the switch tower to pay a visit to Mr. Carter. He sits at rows of lights and black-handled levers, dangerous to touch. Everything up here is dangerous and thrilling. Mr. Carter whittles people, naked people with private parts. Sometimes there are two people stuck together in crazy position. It's quite a museum up here. When the lift-gates clang and drop and the traffic piles up, we all look down on the open automobiles, girls in bathing suits going to the beach. The tower trembles with the thunder of the freight train.

This figurine of steatite speaks to me. Narrow eyes, thick
lips, flat nose, deep carven beard and hair, deep clover-
pattern of vestment. Chalcolithic of Mohenjo-Daro.

In the junk shop I ask to buy the life-size wooden horse.
It came from a saddler's of the sod-house days. But it's
not for sale except to a museum. We go away, my
daughter and I, with a milking stool, nice near the
fireplace.

6 9

They held a celebration for you, Charles, in Iowa. I was
asked but I regretted. It was the hundredth birthday
of your book, your proper Christian book called
Flowers of Evil. (Or is it THE *Flowers of Evil?* I
never know.) And in that hymnal, how well you made
yourself in the image of Poe — Poe with a cross, that's
what you are, adored of the gangster age. In fact,
aren't you a children's poet? Aren't you the Lewis
Carroll of small vice? Your shabby Wonderland of pus
and giant nipple, your cats and jewels and cheap per-
fumes, your licking Lesbians and make-believe Black
Mass, O purulence of Original Sin. And always playing
it safe in the end, like Disneyland. So many safety
devices, pulleys, cranks, classical Alexandrines. It's Iowa
for you, restless spirit, where elderly ladies embezzle
millions in the *acute gratuite.* You'll need no naturali-
zation papers here. And yet I loved you once, and
Delacroix and Berlioz — all in my gangster age. The
little boy in me loved you all, O solemn Charles, so

photogenic. And this is my flower for your anniversary. I fashioned it of Mexican tin and black nail polish, little French Swinburne burning in Iowa City.

5 9

Collecting oneself is like moving to another country. Take this, store that. This poem may come in handy in Kansas. There's one for curious rabbis and young girls. To scramble the chronology make an A B C arrangement. Start with Adam and Eve (to read last at recitals). Is it as much as you thought? There is never enough and never little enough.

Photograph album lying on the grass, the wind reads you lazily. The wind thumbs my episodes. A few drops of rain splatter my years. There's plenty of sighing for impossibles. I love the wine stains on certain accidental poems, pale purple Matisse wallpaper. Who spilled that? Some faces are already repressed. Here is a fallen hand, poked by a stick. The usual insectivora worry my pocket watch. Plenty of castration symbols (you know what *that* means). Dirty-dog poems baying at the moon-mother. Dedicated to three nicknames.

9 6

Balcony Scene

You have beautiful Middle Western legs.

Widow-woman, why on Memorial Day, you who love white, did your bathing suit turn black? Woman in

naked white and black. He dove down the billion-dol-
lar plane, hand at the juke-box switches. The Christmas
tree was clicking in the window. Grief I never heard.
Your children walk on the soft excellent grass. Peonies
lean their hairdos fatly, hands on hips.

Fatlady, I love your face, sort of slapped together. And
   when you walk (white bathing suit, black) it's as if
   one hip, the right, for instance, were going out of joint,
   but to return, a throwing motion, throwing-away, a
   generosity. You bend from the vertical, raising your
   bottom to the blazing sky.

Sunburn. Happy the widow with a hard white ass and a
   willow tree. O pickpock moon, subject of all lost poems,
   birthplace of tides et cetera, true bottom of the sea
   et cetera, O wallsocket.

Vacation

Goldness and whiteness of woman, like a Grand Rapids
   bed or a Sunday paper of brides. The bride coated
   with powder stands in the strongest light at last. She
   is clean. — The sculptor sets his jaw and drives to the
   junk yard. There he can breathe.

Love on the deathbed, love deeper than sunset. The Bros.
   are coming. What! is it nothing but that? Is love
   nothing but that? Battle of Waterloo, nothing but
   that? Fraulein, allumeuse? Or to end a sentence with
   a preposition?

Six cases of bourbon returned to the caterer and the
flowers divided, Hymen hymenaee.

Man with the lamp, hands of ferroconcrete, vellum of
hand, the skin as soft as kid. Big black flashlight, size
of a horsecock, mother's gift. Night silent as hand-
writing, night with two cats on long thin ropes. The
leather coat of early night on the great wet lakes.
Woman, homo normalis!

Consider also their baths, their bows, their brown blood,
their pots, their stenches, out of which the greatest of
sonnet cycles.

WILLIAM STAFFORD *was born in Hutchinson,*
Kansas, and received his B.A. and M.A. degrees at the
state university, and his doctorate at the University of
Iowa. West of Your City, *his first collection, was pub-*
lished in 1960, and Traveling Through the Dark *(1962)*
won the National Book Award in 1963. In the following
year he received the Shelley Memorial Award, and in
1966 a Guggenheim Fellowship. His most recent volume
is The Rescued Year. *For a number of years he has been*
teaching English literature at Lewis and Clark College,
with intervals at Manchester College and San Jose State
College. Known to be one of the most prolific poets in
the United States, his work appears regularly in such
periodicals as Altantic Monthly, Harper's, The New
Yorker *and* The Nation, *and he is represented in a num-*
ber of anthologies.

TIME'S EXILE

From all encounters vintages ensue,
bitter, flat, or redolent. When we met
sunflowers were in bloom.
They mark the highway into Kansas yet.

My unreal errands, once the sun goes down,
fade into streetlight shadows.
Extenuate as the bright lights will, they run
into the hometown shadows.

I'm alongside old happenings when they flare;
like the dog that found the wounded quail
that came up through breast-feather shadows
into the sights and set their wings and sailed

The proximate field, and melted with shot
into another field — I bring things back from everywhere.
I am a man who detours through the park,
a man like those we used to meet back there —

Whose father had a son,
who has a son,
who finds his way by sunflowers through the dark.

PRAIRIE TOWN

There was a river under First and Main;
the salt mines honeycombed farther down.
A wealth of sun and wind ever so strong
converged on that home town, long gone.

At the north edge there were the sandhills.
I used to stare for hours at prairie dogs,
which had their town, and folded their little paws
to stare beyond their fence where I was.

River rolling in secret, salt mines with care
holding your crystals and stillness, north prairie —
what kind of trip can I make, with what old friend,
ever to find a town so widely rich again?

Pioneers, for whom history was walking through dead
    grass,
and the main things that happened were miles and the
    time of day —
you built that town, and I have let it pass.
Little folded paws, judge me: I came away.

TORNADO

First the soul of our house left, up the chimney,
and part of the front window went outward — pursued
whatever tore at the chest. Part of the lake
on top guyed around the point, bellied
like a tent; and fish like seeds ripened felt
a noiseless Command around their gills, while
the wheatfields crouched, reminded with a hand.

That treble talk always at the bottom of the creek
at the mouth, where the lake leaned away from the rock
at the mouth, rose above water. Then Command moved
away again and our town spread, ruined

but relieved, at the bottom of its remembered air.
We weren't left religion exactly (the church
was ecumenical bricks), but a certain tall element:
a pulse beat still in the stilled rock
and in the buried sound along the buried mouth of the
    creek.

CONSERVATIVE

Indiana felt the ice,
yet holds wide lakes against that pain:
I lived in Indiana once,
put these hands into those lakes
of counties near Fort Wayne.

You come a river, then our town
where summer domes the elms that hide
the river, which — a lurking home —
reflects in windows all the clouds
that drift that countryside.

All you that live your city way:
you cannot hold thought ways to hold
the old way steady; nowadays
you cannot hear the songs we sang
or know what glaciers told,

So I'll say this, then stand apart,
allegiant to where we lived
all the way to cross my heart:
Your years — these riffles atoms made —
and your map river-carved

Conceal a map new glaciers plan,
and there are rivers yet to come,
wide lakes again, and maybe hands
to dip like mine, a voice to say:
"For towns, I'll take this one."

IN RESPONSE TO A QUESTION

The earth says have a place, be what that place
requires; hear the sound the birds imply
and see as deep as ridges go behind
each other. (Some people call their scenery flat,
their only picture framed by what they know:
I think around them rise a riches and a loss
too equal for their chart — but absolutely tall.)

The earth says every summer have a ranch
that's minimum: one tree, one well, a landscape
that proclaims a universe — sermon
of the hills, hallelujah mountain,
highway guided by the way the world is tilted,
reduplication of mirage, flat evening:
a kind of ritual for the wavering.

The earth says where you live wear the kind
of color that your life is (gray shirt for me)
and by listening with the same bowed head that sings
draw all into one song, join
the sparrow on the lawn, and row that easy
way, the rage without met by the wings
within that guide you anywhere the wind blows.

Listening, I think that's what the earth says.

BEFORE THE BIG STORM

You are famous in my mind.
When anyone mentions your name
all the boxes marked "1930's"
fall off the shelves;
and the orators on the Fourth of July
all begin shouting again.
The audience of our high school commencement
begins to look out of the windows at the big storm.

And I think of you in our play —
oh, helpless and lonely! — crying,
and your father is dead again.
He was drunk; he fell.

When they mention your name,
our houses out there in the wind
creak again in the storm;
and I lean from our play, wherever I am,
to you, quiet at the edge of that town:
"All the world is blowing away."
"It is almost daylight."
"Are you warm?"

THE ONLY CARD I GOT ON MY
BIRTHDAY WAS FROM AN
INSURANCE MAN

On upland farms into abandoned wells
on a line meridian high
state by state my birthday star comes on
and peers, my birthday night,

and in my eyes it stands while past its light
the world and I turn, just and far, till
every well scans over the year like spokes
of a wheel returning the long soft look of the sky.

Star in a well, dark message: when l die,
my glance drawn over galaxies,
all through one night let a candle nurse the dark
to mark this instant of what I was,
this once — not putting my hand out
blessing for business' sake any frail markers
of human years: we want real friends or none;
what's genuine will accompany every man.

Who travel these lonely wells can drink that star.

ADULTS ONLY

Animals own a fur world;
people own worlds that are variously, pleasingly, bare.
And the way these worlds *are* once arrived for us kids
        with a jolt,
that night when the wild woman danced
in the giant cage we found we were all in
at the state fair.

Better women exist, no doubt, than that one,
and occasions more edifying, too, I suppose.
But we have to witness for ourselves what comes for us,
nor be distracted by barkers of irrelevant ware;
and a pretty good world, I say, arrived that night

when that woman came farming right out of her clothes,
by God,

At the state fair.

THE PETERS FAMILY

At the end of their ragged field
a new field began:
miles told the sunset that Kansas
would hardly ever end,
and that beyond the Cimarron crossing
and after the row-crop land
a lake would surprise the country
and sag with a million birds.

You couldn't analyze those people —
a no-pattern had happened to them:
their field opened and opened,
level, and more, then forever,
never crossed. Their world went everywhere.

LONG DISTANCE

Sometimes when you watch the fire
ashes glow and gray
the way the sun turned cold on spires
in winter in the town back home
so far away.

Sometimes on the telephone
the one you hear goes far
and ghostly voices whisper in.
You think they are from other wires.
You think they are.

ROBERT SWARD *grew up in Chicago, graduated
from the University of Illinois, studied at the Bread
Loaf School of English, and received an M.A. in 1958
from the University of Iowa. He has been Poetry Fellow
at the Bread Loaf Writers' Conference, has studied in
England (1960-61) on a Fulbright grant, and has traveled
and lived briefly in Wales, France and Greece. In 1964
he received a Guggenheim Fellowship in Poetry and in
1966 the University of New Mexico's D.H. Lawrence
Fellowship. His poems have appeared in leading periodi-
cals, and he has published three volumes —* Uncle Dog
and Other Poems *(London, 1962),* Kissing the Dancer &
Other Poems *(1964), and* Thousand-Year-Old Fianceé &
Other Poems *(1965). He has taught at the University of
Iowa, Connecticut College, and Cornell University.*

WALDHEIM CEMETERY

We are in Chicago's Waldheim cemetery.
I am walking with my father.
My nose, my eyes,
    left pink wrinkled oversize
        ear
My whole face is in my armpit.

We are at the stone beneath which lies
My father's mother;
There is embedded in it a pearl-shaped portrait.
I do not know this woman.
    I never saw her.
I am suddenly enraged, indignant.
I clench my fists; I would like to strike her.
My father weeps.
He is Russian; he weeps with
        conviction, sincerity, enthusiasm.
I am attentive.
I stand there listening beside him.
After a while, a little bored,
        but moved,
I decide myself to make the effort;
I have paid strict attention;
I have listened carefully.
Now, I too will attempt tears;
        they are like song,
        they are like flight.
    I fail.

TERMINAL THEATER

We fight. I am clubbed from behind. They pin me
And take turns, forearm feet fists to face
Forefinger and thumb opening eyelids, press
Graze with the nail, touch with the palps
Squash, the Jew's eyes seeing eye, sand
Sprinkle, candlewax, cigarette ash,
Cigar smoke. It is necessary to see this

Against a backdrop of —
For four miles west of it one can smell
The lake; further, it being July, the water
Tastes of chlorine stale fish breath snail-dew
Sharks

Even at nine or ten o'clock, the buildings
Give off an unexpected heat; it has rained
This day, and the night before. I have spent them
At the movies, watching Bud Abbott and Lou Costello
Weary stark flat slapstick, but offering conditions
Questions, occasions for grieved analyses.
Do you not laugh, do you not cry?
What is real? cried the oyster, glob of spit
In a pane of glass.

ALL THE MORNINGS

All the mornings, always pennies
Of my life
Nickels, dimes
    shafts of light, clouds
Have begun
      over things — an alley,
Bushes, pawnshops,
      people.

It is a part of fish, rent-
    stench
Curtain smells,
      tenements
    to be three, four

Five flights above the street,
Over what in the good years
Of a good war one falls on
     now and then,
          dreams on, dies, a park.

All the evenings, always
          streetlights
Buildings, trees
     sculptured out of stone
          Moon
Nickels, dimes
     I'm falling,
          slowly
Quite slowly, now, down
Into the shafts of light.

SCENES FROM A TEXT

"Several *actual*, potentially and/or really
traumatic situations are depicted on these pages."
     — *Transient Personality Reactions to Acute*
          or Special Stress (Chapter 5).

PHOTO I

The car, a '39 Ford,
Lies on its side, windshield smashed
Doors off, bodies strewn, blood, brains
And tow-truck. A boy, perhaps
A girl, rushes about on fire,

And appears to have been so,
Now, for several moments. — Small,
Hairless, and with a face like
Sleep. In his bare, smoking arms
He carries a woman's head.
She is smiling, and her hair
Is all on fire. She too
Appears to be asleep. And the boy
Suddenly presses his head
                        down, *hard*
Into her neck,
            twists, and wears the head backwards.

PHOTO II

The house is burning. The furniture
Is scattered on the lawn (tables, chairs
TV, refrigerator). Momma —
There is a small, superimposed white
Arrow pointing at her — is busy
Tearing out her eyes. The mute husband
(Named, arrowed) stands idly by, his hands
Upon his hips, eyes already out.
The smoke blankets the sky. And the scene,
Apart from Momma, Poppa, the flames . . .
Could be an auction. Friends, relatives
Neighbors, all stand by, reaching, fighting
For the mirrors, TV, sunglasses;
The children, the cats and speechless dogs.

PHOTO III

The scene is an illuminated
Hole. Soldiers, firemen, are descending
(With axes, helmets) the nine ladders.
The moon watches over the shoulders
Of the crowd. Menninger, Murrow, wear earphones.
Unseen, asleep, awake, eighteen hundred feet
Down (where she has fallen, descended to
Willingly, confusing "up" and "down"),
With an NBC tape recorder,
— Instantly, specially lowered to her —
And companionable microphone
The woman is rhythmically, for the
Moment, cursing, annihilating
Us all
          . . . the thick, dream-lost, echoing voice
That one hears as one would hear one's own
(Oneself in a pit, cursing, pleading
Asleep, one's mind become as the earth,
Raging, damning, still, still, still, still, still,
An hysterical stone upon one)
— With indifference, interest, wonder
Or death
          . . . the scene stills, and is a photo.

PHOTO IV

Three men in a canoe, in a flood;
Houses floating upsidedown, children,
Dogs, car-roofs, visible just beneath
The surface of the water. The men

Are dressed in raincoats, hats, faces, eyes:
All of which are composed of water.
Shadows. Water. Black and white water.
The sky, the floating, clapboard houses,
Are also composed of water. A scream!
The man's mouth is the sound of water;
The silence, swirling, the look of it.
It disappears, merges with his face.
And the leaden, still, almost churning
Wake, separate, identical with the flood,
Extends from the canoe back, ten,
Twenty, a thousand yards, to a house
Floating, still, in the distance. Shingled,
White, wooden water, a house of water.
(Like no, like all other houses, *death.*)
— A man, the one man with a paddle,
Begins drinking the scene, the water . . .
The other men, their raincoats, hats and eyes.
He becomes them, and the entire scene.
And all there is, is water, shadows
Water — or what might appear to be
Sleep, water, the inside of one's head.

MY STUDENTS

It is them. I jump up and down hard
Very glad to see them. Jesus Christ.
They whistle, hoot, applaud, proud of me.
Then for hours, days, semesters, weeks
I do not say anything. It happens
Early in September. I break off

In the middle of something. And I stop.
I have nothing more to say to them.
They accept the fact. And are patient.
Meanwhile, I allow them to smoke.
At any time I may start in again. I sense
Their faith in me. And the Word is not yet,
Will not take hold, is not upon me.

MISS ELDERLI DORA
DES MOINES — ONE MARCH

She began to blow away, and put her soft
Kernel lace starch of a palm to her hat;
It was soon against a cloud, and she
Blew beyond the highest stalks, beyond it.

The wind was as if it were the sky, wanting
To get blue back about itself, up up
Up, and away . . . d'Iowaed she went, higher
Than the highest tassels ever reached.

How-dee'do? bowed God, as the harmonicas
Were polkachomp-reeded forth, together
With an old gee-tar (Chaw! Oops!!),
In the sweetcorn-tune . . . softstrummed silk.

ELM TREES

Down hill, the elm trees
In the sunlight,
Their trunks darkish
Under branches, under leaves.

Higher up the hill
In this woman's arms
I see through to the other side
As into another season,
The sun suddenly all
On one side of the leaves.

TURNPIKE

It was a hole, a leveled, paved, black, white hole
A green hole, a blue hole, grass, sky, billboards, air
And we were in the hole — into the air, trees
Grass . . . into what were the trees, the sky, in us.
And we were in the air, the hole that went through
Itself.
    All around us there was what we were
Passing through, inside, inside, inside ourselves.
And the hole was humming, clear, laned, green and
        paved
With black stripes. And there was nothing, the minutes
Miles when you thought of them, when they made you
        them,
The Buick, the speed, the dead skunks at the skunk-
Crossing, the deer — *I pressed down on the horn,*
My hand became a fist, became a sound, a hole
At the end of my wrist, braked *and the thing was dead.*

*   *   *

So, said Death, the deer, sitting there, between us,
With the great, white butterfly — and we were off,

Riding through air, through trees, through grass
   . . . and we were
In the hole, and over the hole, and the hole
Went on forever, into the trees, grass, the sky
That was there, within us, paved, black, white, a rock
A ghost, a Buick-thing, turnpike . . . a token.

JAMES TATE *was born in Kansas City, Missouri,
and received a B.A. in English from Kansas State College
(Pittsburg) in 1965. His first book* The Lost Pilot *was the
Yale Series of Younger Poets choice for 1966, and he has
published poems in a number of magazines, including*
Atlantic Monthly, Shenandoah, North American Review,
Boston Review, *and* Dust. *Presently he teaches the Un-
dergraduate Poetry Workshop at the University of Iowa.*

INTIMIDATIONS OF AN
AUTOBIOGRAPHY

I am walking a trail
on a friend's farm
about three miles from

town. I arrange the day
for you. I stop and say,
you would not believe how happy

I was as a child,
to some logs. Blustery wind
puts tumbleweed

in my face as I am
pretending to be on my way
home to see you and

the family again,
to touch the orange
fingers of the moon.

That's how I think of it.
The years flipped back last night
and I drank hot rum till

dawn.
It was a wild success and I wasn't sad when
I woke past noon

and saw the starlings in the sky.
My brain's an old rag anyway,
but I've got a woman and you'd say

she's too good for me. You'd call
her a real doll and me a goof-ball.
I've got my head between my paws

because it's having a damn
birthday party. How old do you think I am?
I bet you think I'm

seventeen.
It doesn't matter. Just between
us, you know what I'm doing

now? I'm calling the cows home.
They're coming, too.
I lower

myself to the ground lazily,
a shower of avuncular kisses
issuing from my hands and lips —

I just wanted to tell you
I remember you even now;
Goodbye, goodbye. Here come the cows.

UNCLE

Homer was a ventriloquist;
so drunk, one day he projected his voice
so far it just

kept going and going (still is).
Joe Ray insisted
Homer was afraid of work, but he's

had 130 jobs or more
just recently, he didn't think in terms
of careers.

The family never
cared for Homer
even after

he ginned himself into a wall
and died balling
with a deaf mute in an empty Kansas City hall.

Joe Ray insisted
Homer would have made a fine dentist
had he kept his mouth shut; that is,

had he lived. Still is
heard about the house
jiggling glasses,

his devoted astral voice coming back.

AUNT EDNA

Aunt Edna of the hills
comes down to give
her sisters chills;

she wears the same
rags she wore
seven years ago,

she smells
the same, she tells
the same hell

is here stories.
She hates flowers,
she hates the glory

of the church she
abandoned for the
glory

of her Ozark cave.
She gave
her sons to the wolves.

THE LOVELIEST WOMAN
IN ALTOONA, IOWA

Tonight the loveliest woman
in Altoona is giving herself
to a dry cleaning apprentice

beneath swings in City Park.
His mustard breath, his life,
is crystallizing as he

manipulates her loins,
imagining competence. And then
it happens: her coveted eggs

rush through the earth
like small, ecstatic animals,
and the Midwest contracts

in horror. There is hardly
a place to stand. The entire
village has gathered

to confirm the mayor's prediction:
Gabriella and Barnaby have
come to an evil end. Smoke,

water and sirens malign
the sky. Surely it will be
broadcast soon that all

is under control, and the elders
will sigh, thinking they
too are under control,

though their lives were exposed
to a crime of passion.
Come see the people writhe.

IN A TOWN FOR WHICH I KNOW NO NAME

I think of your blind odor
too long till I collide with
barbers, and am suspected.

The clerk malingers when I
nod. I am still afraid of
the natural. Even the

decrepit animals,
coveting their papers and
curbs, awake and go breathing

through the warm darkness of
hotel halls. I think that they
are you coming back from the

colossal obscurity
of your exhausted passions,
and dash to the door again.

LATE HARVEST

I look up and see
a white buffalo
emerging from the
enormous red gates
of a cattle truck
lumbering into
the mouth of the sun.
The prairie chickens
do not seem to fear
me; neither do the
girls in cellophane
fields, near me, hear me
changing the flat tire
on my black tractor.
I consider screaming
to them; then, night comes.

THE END OF THE LINE

We plan in partial sleep
a day of intense activity —
to arrive at a final bargain

with the deaf grocer,
to somehow halt a train;
we plan our love's rejuvenation

one last time. And then
she dreams another life
altogether. I've gone away.

The petals of a red bud
caught in a wind between
Hannibal and Carthage,

the day has disappeared.
Like a little soap bubble
the moon glides around

our bed. We are two negroes
lugubriously sprawled
on a parched boardwalk.

THE SUNDAY DRIVER IN
SEARCH OF HIMSELF

Rolling at eighty, now ninety,
I know why I came here: I was
beginning to feel like a crowd,

you know the ones pinching
each other's fanny, tubercular
wheezing when you turn around.

Whole burping galaxies
of these silly people collecting
inside of me, squeaking,

reeling, until one night, last
night, frozen downtown, I was
trying to recall just where

it was I was going
to meet you, just when, just
who on earth you are. I read

phonebooks, took cabs, waited
in lobbies, ball parks, and
The Tulsa Opera House. Sequinned

ladies, I said, have you seen
the likes of me? Over there,
they said. See, over there.

And, now, here I am, going
lickety-split, hellbound over
mountains, gullies, and water;

and loving, really loving
every mile of it, the knowing
that only you are around.

CHAD WALSH *was born in Virginia but has lived most of his adult life in the midwest. He did graduate work at the University of Michigan, receiving in 1939 an M.A. in French. That year he won the major playwriting award in the Hopwood contests. He went on to receive the doctorate in English in 1943. In 1945 he began teaching at Beloit College, was co-founder (1950) of the* Beloit Poetry Journal *and was for many years one of its editors. He is now Chairman of the Department of English at Beloit, and is also an Episcopal priest. He has published four volumes of poetry —* The Factual Dark, Eden Two-Way, The Psalm of Christ, *and* The Unknowing Dance *— edited* Today's Poets, *and is the author of a college text,* Doors Into Poetry. *He is the first Protestant to receive the annual "Spirit" award of the Catholic Poetry Society of America, and has received an award from the Council for Wisconsin Writers and the Golden Anniversary poetry award of the Society of Midland Authors.*

THE SNOW SHOVEL

It is the first snow of the season, and I am walking home
  from Sears,
Balancing the big badge of my improvidence, 30
  inches wide, guaranteed kind to sedentary backs,
Light weight and expensive as the aluminum trust
  can make them.
The long hill that leads from the Methodist Church
  to the College observatory
Winds white before me; soon I shall be home, and
  the hundred feet of the driveway.

This is a time to ponder the philosophy of hard
      work, to plan a blank verse meditation
Lauding the life of simple toil, and the character
      built by moving snow three feet from where it
      fell,
And if the Puritan heritage that flows in all American
      veins,
Even those whose names end in *-ini*, *-ski*, and *-strom*,
Were not so sluggish in me this overcast day,
I would almost believe I believed it.

But the cost of the shovel and the angle of the hill
      and the length of the driveway
Impart to my mind today a cold biblical clarity; when
      my brow sweats, and the sweat quickly
      congeals,
I shall sing no songs of the nobility of work, but
      rather accept, with what meekness I can, the
      standard curse that Adam contrived for me
      without asking my leave.

I find it sometimes wonderfully refreshing to tell the
      truth. Not many people enjoy this luxury.
That is one of the reasons the Bible is more bought
      and admired and translated than read.
Let me continue and tell some more truth.

Paradise is a Polynesian island, precisely as the
      romantics have always known.
The fruit falls to the ground at the exact moment of
      ripeness, and the few yards of walking to pick
      it up are a pleasant stroll in the climate that is
      attached;

In paradise you eat fruit, write poetry, make love,
    and say your prayers,
Four activities, and almost the only four, that are
    self-validating;
This is the truth, but the other truth is that we do
    not live in paradise; we live in Wisconsin;
The white flakes of the ancient curse are new as
    today's *Beloit Daily News;*
I shall shovel the driveway, put the car to bed,
Read *The New Yorker,* play folksong on the alto
    recorder, and retire from thinking.

SPIRITUAL BIOGRAPHY

No sooner said or done, the word or deed,
Than memory mythologized it. He'd
Convey it safely to his room and test
It for the sins so subtle when confessed
They rang like virtues. Morning-after heads
And crude carnality of bouncing beds
Were not for him. He ate Augustine's pears
And classified their seeds in frequent prayers.
(Father O'Brien heard his voice with terror,
And ladled penances by trial and error.
"Sweet Mary, give me Micks that beat their wives,"
He said, "or Wops too free with carving knives."

He died, he died. It was as he expected —
Not welcomed home nor finally rejected.
His stay in Purgatory lasted ages;
His monologues would fill ten thousand pages;

St. Peter's agents, whom he often met,
Invariably reported back, "Not yet."
The population ebbed and flowed, and he
Progressed in conscience and seniority
Until one day a spirit newly come,
And reeking still of nicotine and rum,
Told him a good one of a farmer's daughter.
He laughed. He paled. He laughed again. The water
Of clear humility rained down his skin,
Dissolved the lucent sheath of subtle sin.
(St. Peter's sides were aching when he let him in.)

SUBURBAN VISTA

Living as we did in one of the nicer suburbs
With an A & P next to the second stop-light,
Even a church for those who cared for such things,
We seldom had need to visit the historic city.

Dimly we remembered the cars advancing, receding
In the parallel veins and arteries of four-lane highways.
Delicatessens and department stores found the stop-light.
Perhaps as a child I went one time to the city.

We have had trouble-makers — collectors of folklore,
Waylayers of old men at the psychosomatic clinic,
Probers, explorers with knapsacks and Geiger counters,
Who strode down the grassy concrete to find a city.

Some of them stumbled home, to haunt us and tell us
How near they approached to the vitrified lawn where
    the statehouse
Stood. But our water and gas mains generally function,
And we hanged the alarmists high high from the
    vibrating stop-light.

THEY WALK UNDER LADDERS

They walk under ladders and joke with black cats.
They knock on many doors but never on wood.
By preference they choose hotels with a thirteenth floor.
They beget 1.3 children per pair, and send it
To a progressive school where creativity is compulsory.
During the Easter holidays they recommend *The Golden
    Bough.*

They often remain married; they have sex twice a week;
They carry 20-40- insurance; they join the AAA.
Sometimes they wonder if Vedanta perhaps is the
    answer.

They publish their memoirs at the age of fifty-two.
They specify cremation or a cemetery with horizontal
    monuments.
They look at gray hairs in a broken mirror.
They read Gayelord Hauser; they eat yogurt;
The face in the mirror forgets to smile back.

from EROS AND AGAPE

4

The massacre of solar hydrogen
To warm our blood is a mad, spendthrift thing.
In a system planned by provident men
Summer would be a lengthened name for spring;
The old wastrel, that sun, he would be rationed
In his consumption of his vital core
So a few extra centuries of us could be stationed
On the earth to shiver a few centuries more.

Still, sitting out here with you in the patio,
Naked as the neighbors up the hill will permit,
Inwardly, outwardly, dually aglow,
I'll let him squander the patrimony a bit
Of my blood claimants in the $n + n$ degree.
I'll never see them, and they'll never see me.

20

When the unnatural warm fair October
Ended and a cold rain made the lawns muddy
Our vague disquiet ceased. Wintry and sober
We braced for snow, and weather-stripped the study.
But now the sun, blue sky, hot days returning
(November, though Wisconsin) we play young.
Dry leaves have no monopoly of burning.
Songs, decades forgotten, burn on my tongue.

One is always at home for what reprieves
The warden brings, nor does one controvert
The Governor's signature. Shakespearean leaves

Hang still in packets, and your April skirt
Is brighter than a hill of maple trees.
Unlike the doomed, we burn before we freeze.

22

To the left, cliffs; the shore where cottages
End with the road; mountain ascents of berries
For the valiant; antlers between the trees;
Tracks of a bear or two (the story varies).
To the right, fields studded with placid cows;
Fences in love with trees like English hedges;
Apple orchards with downward arching boughs;
Farm children diving from the low, bright ledges.

And we possess all shores as our canoe
Glides the long oval of the constant lake;
World upon world that folds into our view,
And fades like shifting bubbles in our wake.
We've made our choice for two abiding things:
Love and a lake refreshed by hidden springs.

FOR DAMARIS,
ABOUT TO BE MARRIED

From an airplane, yes,
One might have seen, as on a colored map,
The little stream in baby turbulence
Rising from a common foothill spring,
Widening with the miles,
Deepening,
And making always for the promised sea.

But I followed, walking,
Fringed by water and the wilderness;
I never saw beyond the closest turning;
And there were times its banks drew close together,
And days of backward eddies.
It did not always
Make for wideness and the rumored sea.

Now in your certain eyes
I read the aerial map of nineteen years
And know the clean proportions of your space.
Now in your eyes I see the homing light
That in another's eyes
Brought me home
Into the ocean where the rains are born.

RELIGIOUS EMPHASIS WEEK

I have come here, knowing before I came
How it would be: eager, helpful committees,
Official luncheons, chitchat in the Grill,
Bull sessions dorm by dorm at half-past ten;
My mind is stocked with true and tested answers —
Irenic words to please the absent Buddhists,
While lauding Trinitarian mathematics.
It is the soft sell, the gentle, bland approach.
Even in convo, thirty minutes a morning,
I'll circle for a day or two, exploring
Literary and sociological fringes
Before I lunge for the theological kill.

I could do better if I felt more bleakly
How damned they are. But Spring's a heretic.
They are so beautiful — not the girls only —
Saga-fair, scrubbed, no smell, or sweet to smell —
The men are lovely, as young animals
All are, until a certain age. By Spring
I am undone, redone, done in, done for.
Sin is as hypothetical as all
This talk of neutrons, protons, other-*ons*
The priests of the sterile white habits insist
Are part and parcel of my solid poundage.

Suppose, next morning, if Spring is really here,
After the student-led devotion, after
The introduction, I took my collar off
And sent it sailing like a flighty token
Of Mardi Gras, and in the pause intoned,
"Dearly beloved, ye lovers and ye loved,
Let us defrock all presidents, and deans
Of every species, counselors, house mothers;
Assemble in a pleasant grove, elect
A King and Queen of Love, dance in a ring,
Fashion a form of Cupid, wreathe it, erect it
Upon the altar of the Unknown God
Whom Spring reveals when you unveil by two's."

If I should lose (see Freud) the manuscript
I brought with me, I'm really scared I'll do it.
I do not think they will elect me King
But if they do, can I refuse to reign?

JOHN WOODS *was born in Martinsville, Indiana, and educated at the state university and the University of Iowa. Since 1955 he has taught at Western Michigan University, where he is Professor of English, concentrating on creative writing and contemporary literature. He served as poetry consultant for Indiana University Press and as poetry editor for the Aural Press. He has recorded for the Library of Congress and Fenn College Poetry Center, was a Robert Frost Fellow in Poetry at the Bread Loaf School of Writing and has worked at the Yaddo and MacDowell writers' colonies. He has published three volumes —* The Deaths at Paragon, Indiana; On the Morning of Color; *and* The Cutting Edge. *He is represented in a number of anthologies and appears regularly in leading periodicals, among them,* Poetry Magazine, Kenyon Review, Chicago Review, Poetry New York, *and* The Folio.

THE VISITS OF MY AUNT

The visits of my aunt in Martinsville
Were invasions. I see the webby arbor
And the tottered shed full of kindling
And games, the willow lacing the pause
Of afternoon, and townsmen rocking
Under wasp shells and locust husks.
Then my aunt's car would startle dogs
To ragged challenges as she blew her horn
Down Grant Street. Puffing out onto the yard
With a moustache and blue-wet dress,

She hugged me breathless. Her car door
Slammed down birds from the carved maple.
The keepsakes would jump when she sat:
The plaster horse and carnival cane,
The one ashtray kept for her flourishes.
Our latest uncle tugged the creases
In his pants and face, and tapped his watch.
Summer ventured in her voice.
That rusting crankcase filled with rain,
Half-hidden in the weeds, held no
More rainbow than she stroked from air.
The steaming dump up Lincoln Road,
With rats and springs, held no more
Oddness than her pocketbook
To trick us with. While she spoke
Clouds held their rain, and August
Lay like lambs beneath her spell.
The piano repeated, deep in its harps,
Her essential hum.

When she died,
Under the glass tent, I grew into an answer:
That life, as well as death, can last forever.
There is a heaven of things: car doors,
Uncles, the ashtray from the Exposition.
But as she withered in the tilted bed,
I came with the first frost to another meaning:
Something of brown leaves, withered grapes,
The ganged birds exploding from the oak;
That someday the easy wind would knot,
And I'd be helpless in the grip of days.

BERT IN THE ORCHARD

Mrs. Carter, glasses hanging from her eyes,
Hated orchards. She rapped her buggy
Past my trees. This turned me, collared
In a chalky Sunday school, away from psalms.
For I had seen her pinned beneath
The preacher on the choir stage; the moon
Squared on their secret thighs, glancing
Pitilessly on their placed eye glasses.

It led me from the preacher's words, bending
His wooden voice over the swayed congregation
Like a windy oak, until chandeliers leaned
From the gale, and the church hove to
In the calm collection. He read a book,
But the words were windfall, and full
Of troubles. O Mrs. Carter, what
Winds of the groin blew me to your arms?

I had not thought of her till now. Fog
Slipped from Indian Creek, bandaging
The near trees. I felt the juices settling
In the fruit, and heard the quarry coughing
Across Nutter's Hill; and I remembered
Slow seasons in her laugh, and felt
Tongues of Eve playing madness on my teeth.
Apples claimed me. I dangled, red and full.

I moved among the trees, eddying fog,
Among the forming apples, deep in green.
Here is where I brought my love to kiss.
Fifty years, Mrs. Carter, and now I think

Of you, and dab at mulch with my boot,
Sensing the old chemistry that sun forces
Through the winding roots, embracing
With frail green the bones of something.

NIGHT CONSTABLE

1

An old man, shaking the doors. See him
Preceded by a dog. Have him not
Part of the dark or greened by neon.
See the streets stride out from under him,
And lights turn their wheels around his path.
I would have him looking in, staining
The glass with his wordless breath.
Nor is this dog more than the mission
Of its bark, the avid tongue steaming
Over water, the cabalistic circle
Before reclining, a summer's great digging.

He slept at day, blinds drawn around him,
In a green sluice like swimmers in a pool.
Dreams like bubbles lifted from his face:
Something of fruit rotting in a cellar
With subtle exhalation of steam, delayed
Harvest festering; that which cannot happen,
Or having happened, cannot mean.

2

Once he loved beeplace and cambered leaf,
Thick rocks notching the water, a house
Bulging with quiet, trees where
                              "a bird gays,"
She said; "its heart breathes a circling fire."
They swam in August at the gravel pit.
Numb with sun, they knew the heaven in the flesh,
The saving kiss, the missionary hands.
With maps of water, they explored experience.
Eyes opened, they swam below the water
In a dream of color, in a holding air:
Slow, laboring birds, near, retreating.
Bubbles like dreams lifted from their twisting
Mouths, to speak the summer out above.
Open wide, their bodies moved
                              along the weeds
And cloyed fronds, his thought dragged along
The bottom. Roots grew up and tangled
In his dredging mind. O the fruits
That fall or cannot fall in dreaming gardens.
There the sucking root is flower and fruit.

3

Doors and locks his one concern when night
Slid down from under his lids. As he walked
His compass out, he saw an empty world:
The shop with nothing but a sign alive,
Where suited dummies stared him down; the bar
With chairs turned up, the bottles blinking,
And no laughter in the shadowed glass. See him

Set back on his heels by fat and age, ingrown,
Emptied of weathers, see him shaking the doors.

Think a scene of
               dark, the searchlights crossed
Above the gravel pit. He could see the grappling
Hooks churn up muddy weeds, the ah-ing watchers,
The tower from which she dived. Deeper, deeper
Still, her body shrinking as she sank
Beyond his doors, his love, beyond forgetting.

THE LAST RESORT

I am losing. The ragged pier
Goes diving in the bulging lake.
Only weather rents my skiffs.
We settle in the mud. Night
Gaps the string of colored lights
Around the lake. Dark reaches in.
Each day I shed a breath, closer
To shambles, my hands as empty as when
I reached for eggs upon a nest
Wind untied. O I can't keep.

Once they jostled me outside
And made me dig up gin I'd made.
Inside they stamped the floor with dances.
The class of 1925 tore down
The diving board. Bust me, I was
King of something. But we were left
Behind to web and founder, dropped.

Each day I widen like a puff
To haunt the rafters; only nearest
Pains can hurt me now. The juke box
Twirls its senseless colors nightly.
Nothing dances but a hat of moths
Above the light. The sheriff woke me
Yesterday, scratching the glass.
He'd heard that I was dead. He said
They'd dig me up like jars one day
Along with buggy bones.
                                    But last night
My stork came walking in the shallows,
Treading his image into wheels,
Fishing the moon-draped waters.
O let me widen into nothing.
I'm king of all I see. I'm king
Of all the lovely visibles.

THE DEATHS AT
PARAGON, INDIANA

1. Sandra, the waitress

Sun streaked the coffee urn
And wrote AL'S LUNCH across the cups.
I saw no harm in summer then,
And held against the scorching sun
A spring, touching the deepest earth,
That trickled in the bearded tub
Behind the store. But nothing holds
When fire levels on the frying concrete.

Thermometer said, "Go easy, girl.
Dodge trouble." And so I fed
The truckers, watching the tube of coffee
Twitch along the urn, the street
Repeat itself across the mirror.
I washed an egg beneath the tap.

Then, too sudden for the mind,
The car came rolling, spraying parts
And boys across the road outside.
He came, and comes forever, sliding
Headfirst into the curb, bursting.
The egg broke below my hand.
O this to say: his arm was bent
Behind his back; dust and leaves
Crawled downstream in the gutter.
O this to hope: someday his staring
Eyes will close upon my dream.

2. *Goss, the ambulance driver*

My head goes spinning in the siren,
But I hold the road. Muscles
Keep the old shapes. When oaks
Are ripped by lightning, tip to root,
Will sap spring out until the tree
Hangs wrinkled as an inner tube
From junkyard fences? Dr. Sweet,
This Siren calls: "I am the cross
Your training binds you to." But hear,
One behind is crucified
Upon a steering wheel, and bleeds
His heart away. Sew on him
A year, and he will lie unbuckled.

But now to drive this ambulance
With all my riders emptying
Behind me.
                    O this to say:
Lives are balloons; and when the moorings
Drop, the wind takes you sailing.
Like inner tubes, they round around
Their hold on air. O this to cry:
Someday the wind goes slack, and they
Go spinning like my passengers.

3. Chauncey, the junk man

Scatter me, wind. I am the king
Of bang and rattle, of fall apart
And rust in weeds. Here is where
Things wobble off to. My offerings
Come sailing from back doors: wires
Distracted into sparks, handles
That give you pains, and broken holders.
If I were mayor, every matron
Would come unglued and hit the spot
With all her joints aglow. But I
Can coax a shape in anything,
And make it stick, and tend and solder.

O this to say: today I dragged
A mash of wheels and sparking sides
Into my shed. First I cluttered
Ledges with all unwired cubes;
Then I festooned rafters with
The unlinked flexible. But when

I gathered shape into my brain,
I cowered under fenders, reeling.
The shape was fall and spin and blast.
The shape was death. I let it go.

4. Doctor Sweet

Yesterday I fished for bass,
But now I fish for breath in bones
Clasped as bottom roots. The pulse
Nibbled like a chub but got
Away. All five of you are dead.
Light beaks my eyes, and edges
My knives with fire. Though I link
You by my chart, you'll dangle empty.
Even Chauncey, with his shed of parts,
Can never make you run. I know
He'll tow your flattened car away
And hang its pieces from his roof
Like sausages and collarbones.
I fear he'd bandage you with earth.

I know those visitors below.
They come to lynch you with their pity.
You left them with their loves and debts,
Responsibility and guilt.
This mob of tears will not forgive.
O now I give you to their hands
For burial in summer's earth.
O this to hope: that you will never
Wake upon an empty world
And cry for love, and hear no answer.

JAMES WRIGHT *was born in Ohio and educated at Kenyon College and the University of Washington. His books of poems are* The Green Wall *(Yale Series of Younger Poets, 1957),* Saint Judas *(1959), and* The Branch Will Not Break *(1963). He has published poems in anthologies and in numerous periodicals, including* Harper's Bazaar, Poetry Magazine. Quarterly Review of Literature, Altantic Monthly, Botteghe Oscure, The Nation, Choice, Big Table, The New Yorker *and in the* Saturday, Kenyon, Hudson, *and* Chicago *reviews. He has taught in Minnesota, presently teaches at Barnard College.*

AS I STEP OVER A PUDDLE AT THE END OF WINTER, I THINK OF AN ANCIENT CHINESE GOVERNOR

And how can I, born in evil days and fresh from failure,
ask a kindness of Fate? — WRITTEN A.D. *819*

Po Chu-i, balding old politician,
What's the use?
I think of you,
Uneasily entering the gorges of the Yang-Tze,
When you were being towed up the rapids
Toward some political job or other
In the city of Chungshou.
You made it, I guess,
By dark.

But it is 1960, it is almost spring again,
And the tall rocks of Minneapolis
Build me my own black twilight
Of bamboo ropes and waters.
Where is Yuan Chen, the friend you loved?
Where is the sea, that once solved the whole loneliness
Of the Midwest? Where is Minneapolis? I can see
    nothing
But the great terrible oak tree darkening with winter.
Did you find the city of isolated men beyond mountains?
Or have you been holding the end of a frayed rope
For a thousand years?

AUTUMN BEGINS IN
MARTINS FERRY, OHIO

In the Shreve High Football stadium,
I think of Polacks nursing long beers in Tiltonsville,
And gray faces of Negroes in the blast furnace at
    Benwood,
And the ruptured night watchman of Wheeling Steel,
Dreaming of heroes.

All the proud fathers are ashamed to go home.
Their women cluck like starved pullets,
Dying for love.

Therefore,
Their sons grow suicidally beautiful
At the beginning of October,
And gallop terribly against each other's bodies.

FEAR IS WHAT QUICKENS ME

1

Many animals that our fathers killed in America
Had quick eyes.
They stared about wildly,
When the moon went dark.
The new moon falls into the freight yards
Of cities in the south,
But the loss of the moon to the dark hands of Chicago
Does not matter to the deer
In this northern field.

2

What is that tall woman doing
There, in the trees?
I can hear rabbits and mourning doves whispering
        together
In the dark grass, there
Under the trees.

3

I look about wildly.

MINERS

1

The police are probing tonight for the bodies
Of children in the black waters
Of the suburbs.

2

Below the chemical riffles of the Ohio River,
Grappling hooks
Drag delicately about, between skiff hulks and sand
    shoals,
Until they clasp
Fingers.

3

Somewhere in a vein of Bridgeport, Ohio;
Deep in a coal hill behind Hanna's name;
Below the tipples, and dark as a drowsy woodchuck;
A man, alone,
Stumbles upon the outside locks of a grave, whispering
Oh let me in.

4

Many American women mount long stairs
In the shafts of houses,
Fall asleep, and emerge suddenly into tottering palaces.

TWO POEMS ABOUT PRESIDENT HARDING

One: His Death

In Marion, the honey locust trees are falling.
Everybody in town remembers the white hair,
The campaign of a lost summer, the front porch
Open to the public, and the vaguely stunned smile
Of a lucky man.

"Neighbor, I want to be helpful," he said once.
Later, "You think I'm honest, don't you?"
Weeping drunk.

I am drunk this evening in 1961,
In a jag for my countryman,
Who died of crab meat on the way back from Alaska.
Everyone knows that joke.

How many honey locusts have fallen,
Pitched rootlong into the open graves of strip mines,
Since the First World War ended
And Wilson the gaunt deacon jogged sullenly
Into silence?
Tonight,
The cancerous ghosts of old con men
Shed their leaves.
For a proud man,
Lost between the turnpike near Cleveland
And the chiropractors' signs looming among dead
mulberry trees,
There is no place left to go
But home.

"Warren lacks mentality," one of his friends said.
Yet he was beautiful, he was the snowfall
Turned to white stallions standing still
Under dark elm trees.

He died in public. He claimed the secret right
To be ashamed.

Two: His Tomb in Ohio

"... *he died* of a busted gut."
— MENCKEN, on Bryan.

A hundred slag piles north of us,
At the mercy of the moon and rain,
He lies in his ridiculous
Tomb, our fellow citizen.
No, I have never seen that place,
Where many shadows of faceless thieves
Chuckle and stumble and embrace
On beer cans, stogie butts, and graves.

One holiday, one rainy week
After the country fell apart,
Hoover and Coolidge came to speak
And snivel about his broken heart.
His grave, a huge absurdity,
Embarrassed cops and visitors.
Hoover and Coolidge crept away
By night, and women closed their doors.

Now junkmen call their children in
Before they catch their death of cold;
Young lovers let the moon begin
Its quick spring; and the day grows old;
The mean one-legger who rakes up leaves
Has chased the loafers out of the park;
Minnegan Leonard half-believes
In God, and the poolroom goes dark;

America goes on, goes on
Laughing, and Harding was a fool.
Even his big pretentious stone
Lays him bare to ridicule.
I know it. But don't look at me.
By God, I didn't start this mess.
Whatever moon and rain may be,
The hearts of men are merciless.

BEGINNING

The moon drops one or two feathers into the field.
The dark wheat listens.
Be still.
Now.
There they are, the moon's young, trying
Their wings.
Between trees, a slender woman lifts up the lovely
      shadow
Of her face, and now she steps into the air, now she is
      gone
Wholly, into the air.
I stand alone by an elder tree, I do not dare breathe
Or move.
I listen.
The wheat leans back toward its own darkness,
And I lean toward mine.

A BLESSING

Just off the highway to Rochester, Minnesota,
Twilight bounds softly forth on the grass.
And the eyes of those two Indian ponies
Darken with kindness.
They have come gladly out of the willows
To welcome my friend and me.
We step over the barbed wire into the pasture
Where they have been grazing all day, alone.
They ripple tensely, they can hardly contain their
    happiness
That we have come.
They bow shyly as wet swans. They love each other.
There is no loneliness like theirs.
At home once more,
They begin munching the young tufts of spring in the
    darkness.
I would like to hold the slenderer one in my arms,
For she has walked over to me
And nuzzled my left hand.
She is black and white,
Her mane falls wild on her forehead,
And the light breeze moves me to caress her long ear
That is delicate as the skin over a girl's wrist.
Suddenly I realize
That if I stepped out of my body I would break
Into blossom.

ABOUT THE EDITOR

Lucien Stryk grew up in Chicago and attended Indiana University, University of Iowa, the Sorbonne, and London University. He has held study grants at Yale University and the University of Chicago, a Fulbright grant in Iran, and has twice been a Visiting Lecturer in Japan. He has taught at writers' conferences in Kentucky and Minnesota, and has given poetry readings at universities throughout the country.

Mr. Stryk has published three books of poetry, Taproot, The Trespasser, Notes for a Guidebook *(New Poetry Series Award), and, with Takashi Ikemoto, a book of Zen Buddhist literature and philosophy —* ZEN: Poems, Prayers, Sermons, Anecdotes, Interviews. *His poems have appeared in a number of anthologies and more than fifty periodicals, ranging from* The Listener *(London) and* Saturday Review *to university quarterlies. In 1963 he shared first prize with John Berryman and Hayden Carruth in the* Chicago Daily News' *New "Chicago" Poem Competition, and in 1964 won* Voices' *Isaac Rosenbaum Poetry Award. At present he teaches poetry, creative writing, and Oriental literature at Northern Illinois University.*

Lightning Source UK Ltd.
Milton Keynes UK
UKHW042224290919
350631UK00011B/3/P